the ultimate
FRYER
COOKBOOK

the ultimate
FRYER
COOKBOOK

WENDY SWEETSER

A QUINTET BOOK

Copyright © 2004 Quintet Publishing Limited.

First edition for North America published in 2004 by
Running Press Book Publishers

9 8 7 6 5 4 3 2 1
Digit on the right represents the number of this printing.

Library of Congress Catalog Card Number: 2004090744

International Standard Book Number: 0-7624-1963-6

Conceived, designed, and produced by
Quintet Publishing Limited
6 Blundell Street
London N7 9BH

Project editor: Catherine Osborne
Art director: Roland Codd
Designer: Rod Teasdale
Photographer: Phillip Wilkins
Food Stylist: Wendy Sweetser

Creative director: Richard Dewing
Publisher: Oliver Salzmann

Manufactured by Provision, Singapore
Printed by SNP Leefung Printers Limited, China

Contents

Introduction

ABOVE Tempura shrimp with barbecue sauce.

There is no escaping the fact that if we want comfort food or a quick, satisfying snack we're probably talking "deep-fried." French fries, doughnuts, fried chicken, and fritters—we love them all—but can't ignore that little voice nagging away inside telling us they're nice but oh! so very, very naughty.

With many of us preoccupied these days with cholesterol, calorie counting, and keeping slim, deep-fried food has attracted a bad press and literally been consigned to the back burner as steaming, dry roasting, and broiling have taken over. Delicious though food is cooked by these methods, it's an inescapable fact that old habits die hard and, for most of us, our cravings for battered fish, crisp-crumbed mushrooms, or thick crunchy French fries don't go away.

But is deep-fried food really so bad for us? The good news is "no" as long as it forms part of a balanced diet. Starvation rations or completely cutting out certain groups of foods may achieve dramatic results in the short term but by depriving yourself of the foods you enjoy can make you crave them all the more, and once you fall off the wagon getting back on will become harder every time. It's much better to continue eating the things you enjoy, but in moderation, so you don't end up feeling deprived.

While nobody can claim that deep-fried food is low cal and suitable for every meal, it can nevertheless form part of a sensible eating plan, as long as the cook follows a few simple rules. Words like "fatty," "heavy," and "soggy" might have given deep-frying a bad name but by making sure you heat oil to the correct temperature, you give food a protective coating, and drain it well before serving, the adjectives shift to "light," "crisp," and "delicious." If deep-fried correctly, food should absorb no more than a couple of tablespoons per 2½ cups of oil—roughly the same as shallow frying.

As a convenient and enjoyable way to cook, deep-frying turns up in almost every national cuisine. India has its samosas and gulab jamun, South East Asian countries prize their tempura, wontons, and spring rolls, and Americans enjoy corn dogs and Southern fried chicken with relish. In Europe each country has its deep-fried treats from French beignets and Spanish churros to Italian fritto misto and great British fish and chips. Cooks have long valued these dishes as an important part of their culinary heritage, as recipes have passed down the generations.

RIGHT Apple funnel cake

If you reluctantly banished your deep fat fryer to the garage several years ago, maybe it's time to dust it off and let it back in the kitchen. The recipes in this book aim to show you that deep-fried food can be part of a sensible, balanced diet, it needn't be over-rich and horribly unhealthy but light, tasty and, there to be enjoyed. So let's get frying tonight!

BE SAFE WHEN DEEP-FRYING

It might be stating the obvious but it is imperative to take extra care when you deep-fry in your kitchen at home. We've all read about the horrific consequences of oil-filled pans catching fire and none of us wants to become one of those statistics.

Electric deep-fat fryers are the safest way to deep-fry as they are solidly built, difficult to tip over, and have a tight-fitting lid that keeps the hot oil covered while the food is cooking. If you have small children, pets that might get under your feet, or you deep-fry regularly, it's well worth investing in one of these.

However, it is perfectly safe to use a saucepan and frying basket as long as you follow a few common sense guidelines:

- Never leave a pan of hot fat unattended. If the phone rings and you've just put food in the fryer, lift the basket clear of the oil, turn off the heat source and continue when you've finished the call (remembering to reheat the oil back up to the correct temperature first).
- Avoid over-filling the saucepan with oil. It should not be more than half-full and there should be roughly 3 inches between the oil and the top of the pan. Remember the oil level will rise when you add food.
- Never carry an open pan of hot fat across the kitchen. Slide the pan carefully to the back of the stove top and leave the fat to cool down.

- When using a saucepan for deep-frying, turn the handle inward so there is no risk of you catching it with your sleeve and overturning the pan.
- Keep a fire extinguisher or fire blanket within easy reach should an accident happen and the oil catch fire. Turn off the heat source and never attempt to put out the fire by dousing it with water as this will cause the flames to spread.
- Avoid putting wet food into hot oil or it will splash and spit.
- If deep-frying in a saucepan, choose a pan where the base is larger than the hot plate so any splashes do not come in contact with an electric hot plate or gas flame.

ABOVE Cooks in Asian countries not only use their wok for stir-frying, but also for creating deep-fried dishes such as crispy seaweed.

TYPES OF DEEP-FRYERS

ELECTRIC DEEP-FAT FRYERS

These vary considerably in size and price but all should have a filter to keep frying odors at bay, a thermostat to heat the oil to the correct temperature, and a basket that can be lowered and raised easily. Other features to look out for are a built-in timer, non-stick coating, viewing window, variable heat control, dishwasher safe basket and interior liner, and a basket that can be lowered and raised without opening the lid.

WOK

In Asian countries, cooks use a wok for every method of cooking including deep-frying. While its unique shape of narrow base and wide top make it ideal for deep-frying, it is essential the rounded bottom of the wok is securely anchored on a special stand so there is no risk of it wobbling or tipping over when filled with hot oil.

LARGE SAUCEPAN WITH FRYING BASKET

The saucepan should be deep and made of either cast iron or thick metal with a heavy bottom. The frying basket should have hooks (or a similar device) that will fit over the top edge of a saucepan allowing excess oil to drip back into the pan before the food is tipped out of the basket and drained on paper towels.

LARGE, DEEP FRYING SKILLET

This can be used for deep-frying small items of food such as croutons or bite-size fritters that only require an inch or so of oil for them to be immersed.

FONDUE SET

Ideal for table cooking when you're planning an informal dinner with friends. As well as the classic fondues of cheese and bourguignon made with beef, the pot can also be used for Japanese tempura.

ABOVE When deep-frying with a wok, make sure it is safely secured to a special stand to avoid wobbling.

RIGHT You don't have to own an electric deep-fat fryer to create delicious fried treats. You can also use a fondue set or a skillet.

WHICH FAT TO USE FOR DEEP-FRYING?

Oil is the most popular fat for deep-frying food, although solid white vegetable fat or lard could also be used. Different oils have different smoke points, i.e., the temperature to which the oil can be heated before it starts to smoke, as follows:

Soy, grape seed, safflower, groundnut (peanut)	-	430°F
Canola	-	405°F
Olive, sesame, corn	-	400°F
Sunflower	-	375°F

Oil marked simply "Vegetable Oil" will be made up of a mix of different oils, e.g., corn, canola, and soy. Excellent for deep-frying, it has a high smoke point, no intrusive flavor and, being a mix of oils, is cheaper than single ingredient oils.

Olive and sesame oils are rarely used for deep-frying because of their strong taste. However, when cooking some Mediterranean or Chinese dishes these oils are used specifically to add their flavor to the dish.

If frying with olive oil, use ordinary olive oil or refined olive oil residue, (oil extracted from the solid residue after olive oil has been pressed out and then refined) both of which have the same smoke and flash points as corn oil and are very stable at high temperatures. Extra virgin olive oils should be avoided as although most are stable at high temperatures some may not be. One of the advantages of ordinary olive oil is that it is actually more stable than other vegetable oils because of its anti-oxidant content (mostly vitamin E), some of which survives the refining process. It can therefore be used more times in a deep-fat fryer than other oils, as long as it is filtered each time to get rid of burnt bits of food and its temperature is thermostatically controlled (see Re-using Oil opposite). Refined olive oil residue does not contain any vitamin E but is still a good oil to deep-fry with and is cheaper than ordinary olive oil.

Although the majority of oils have higher smoke points than 375°F, it is dangerous to heat oil for deep-frying above this temperature. If the oil does get too hot, remove the pan from the heat to allow it to cool to the required temperature. When frying food at high altitudes, the recommended oil temperature should be raised by 25°F.

BELOW There's nothing like cooking your own home-made French fries.

RE-USING OIL

Oil can be re-used several times. After frying, allow the oil to cool completely before draining it through a fine strainer or coffee filter paper to remove any particles of food before pouring it back into the bottle.

If the oil starts to smoke or becomes dark in color, it has been heated to too high a temperature and must be discarded as it will give food an unpleasant burnt flavor. When oil gets too hot, it begins to oxidize and break down, a chemical reaction caused by the heating process.

Fish can taint frying oil especially if it has a strong flavor so, if this happens, keep the oil separate and do not use for frying other foods.

STEPS TO PERFECT DEEP-FRYING

- With the exception of French fries, which are cooked for a brief time, food needs a protective coating before it is deep-fried. This coating will protect delicate ingredients and stop the food absorbing too much oil (see Coatings page 13).
- Food with a high water content, such as fish, should be coated about 30 minutes before frying. Other foods should not be left to stand for too long or the coating will absorb moisture from the food and prevent it becoming crisp.
- Oil needs to be heated to the correct temperature before food can be fried. If your deep-fryer doesn't have a built-in thermostat, it is worth investing in a cooking thermometer. Alternatively, you can calculate the temperature of the oil by adding a cube of bread and checking how long it takes the bread to sizzle and brown. Timings for this method are featured below.

BELOW Spicy samosas make a delicious snack.

Oil temperature	Time it takes bread to sizzle and brown
Low—325°F	60 seconds
Moderate—350°F	40 seconds
Hot—375°F	20 seconds

- Before frying, dip the empty frying basket in the hot oil first so food doesn't stick to it. Cook food in small batches as overfilling the basket will encourage pieces of food to stick together and cause the temperature of the oil to drop. When adding food to the basket, make sure each piece has space around it.
- Add ingredients to hot oil a few pieces at a time using tongs or a similar utensil and avoid dropping anything in from a height as it will cause the oil to rise up in the pan or spit.
- Drain food as soon as it is cooked by placing it on a plate lined with a double thickness of paper towels. When frying in batches, drain the food as it cooks and keep warm (in a single layer) in a low oven with the oven door slightly open so air can circulate. Avoid covering the food as this will create steam and make it go soggy. Dust deep-fried food with salt or sugar to help absorb any oil remaining on the surface.

TROUBLE SHOOTING—WHAT WENT WRONG?

FOOD IS PALE IN COLOR AND COATING HEAVY AND GREASY
- Undercooking
- Food not fried immediately after coating
- Oil not heated to a high enough temperature

FOOD HAS GONE SOGGY
- Food chilled too long before frying
- Food covered while being kept warm

COATING HAS BROWNED TOO MUCH BEFORE
THE FOOD IS COOKED
- Oil has become too hot
- Coating has too much added salt or sugar

FRITTERS OR BEIGNETS BURST
- Oil too hot causing fruit or other filling to burst

COATINGS

A coating is necessary to protect delicate ingredients and stop food absorbing too much oil as it fries. Coatings can be in the form of a batter, breadcrumbs (dry or fresh), matzo meal, dry polenta, seasoned flour, pastry (choux, phyllo, puff, Chinese spring roll wrappers), or semolina.

Batters made with whole eggs are thick and rich, whereas those made with just egg white will be light and crisp.

Before coating with a batter, food should be dusted first with flour so the batter has something to stick to, otherwise most of it will simply slide off. Food with a dry coating such as breadcrumbs, matzo meal, or polenta, needs to be dusted first with all-purpose flour and then brushed with beaten egg before the crumbs are pressed over.

For a dish like Chicken Kiev where it is important the garlic butter and herb filling doesn't leak out during cooking, the chicken breasts are given a double coating of all-purpose flour, beaten egg, and crumbs to ensure a tight seal.

ABOVE Before you place your food in the deep-fat fryer for frying, dip the basket in the oil first so that the food doesn't stick to the wire when you place it in to cook.

BATTERS

All batters (except Tempura batter) should be left to stand for 30 minutes to 1 hour (or longer) before using as this allows the gluten in the flour to swell and gives a lighter batter. If after standing the batter has thickened too much, stir in a little extra water, or beer if it is a beer batter. If adding whisked egg whites, fold these in after the batter has been left to stand.

Tempura Batter

2 egg yolks
1¼ cups (10 fluid ounces) iced water
1¾ cups (7 ounces) all-purpose flour

Put the egg yolks in a bowl and whisk in the water, beating until frothy. Sift in the flour and beat until just combined. The batter should have the consistency of light cream, so if it is too thick add a little more water. As this batter is very light, it should be made and used straight away.

Yeast Batter

¼ -ounce sachet of easy-blend dried yeast
Pinch of sugar
¾ cup (3 ounces) all-purpose flour
½ cup (4 fluid ounces) warm water
¼ cup (2 fluid ounces) warm milk

Sprinkle the yeast and sugar over the flour in a bowl. Stir until well blended. Pour in the water and milk and stir to make a smooth batter. Cover and leave to stand for 1 hour until frothy. Stir before using.

Simple Flour and Water Batter

1¾ cups (7 ounces) self-rising flour
Pinch of baking soda
¼ cup (2 fluid ounces) cold water

Sift the self-rising flour and baking soda into a bowl, make a well in the center and pour in the water. Whisk to make a smooth batter. Leave to stand for 1 hour before using.

Beer Batter—No 1

1 cup (4 ounces) self-rising flour
Pinch of salt
½ teaspoon baking powder
1 cup (8 fluid ounces) light beer

Sift the self-rising flour, salt, and baking powder into a bowl. Make a well in the center and add half the beer. Gradually whisk this into the dry ingredients and then whisk in the rest of the beer until you have a smooth batter. Leave to stand for 1 hour before using.

Beer Batter—No 2

2 cups (8 ounces) self-rising flour
1¼ cups (10 fluid ounces) light beer
Salt and pepper
1 egg white

Sift the self-rising flour into a bowl, make a well in the center and add half the beer. Gradually whisk this into the flour and whisk in the rest of the beer until smooth. Season with salt and pepper. Leave to stand for at least 1 hour. Just before using, whisk the egg white until standing in soft peaks and fold into the batter.

Deep-fried Turkeys

- In recent years, more and more cooks in America's Deep South have begun deep-frying their Thanksgiving turkeys. Fans of this method of cooking say it's fun, easy, and hassle-free and that once you've tasted the moist, succulent flesh of a deep-fried turkey you won't go back to oven-roasting ever again.

- Critics are more cautious, pointing out that deep-frying such a large bird is dangerous and a disaster waiting to happen and regular reports of burns, fires, and serious accidents tend to give credence to their views.

- However, any cooking method for turkey requires care and attention and deep-frying is no different. Stick to the recommended guidelines and safety rules and you can cook a bird this way with confidence.

- For a 10–12 pound turkey you will need a large pot, a high output heat source, and a special long-stem temperature probe, so it's worth investing in a special 36-40 quart fryer from a kitchen equipment store. Each make will come with its own cooking and safety instructions so it is essential to read these before you begin.

- If you buy a frozen turkey, it must defrost completely before it is cooked, partly because any ice crystals left in the body cavity will slow the cooking process down but, more importantly, if you lower a frozen or partly-thawed turkey into hot oil the moisture in it will cause the oil to spit dangerously and boil over.

- To ensure a turkey is completely defrosted, place the bird in its plastic wrapper on a tray in the refrigerator and leave it there for 24 hours for every 5 pounds the bird weighs.

- When ready to deep-fry it, avoid stuffing the turkey and season it instead using a commercially produced spice mix or sauce and injector or your own combination of spices rubbed inside the bird (avoid seasoning the outside of the turkey as this will fall off when it goes into the oil).

- Although the turkey must be completely surmerged in the frying oil, it is imperative not to overfill the fryer as when you lower in the bird, the hot oil could overflow. To calculate how much oil to use, place the turkey in the empty fryer and pour in enough water to cover it by a couple of inches. Lift the bird out and measure the water to determine the quantity of oil you need. Any oil with a high smoke point can be used, although groundnut (peanut) oil is the favorite of many cooks who say its flavor best compliments the turkey flesh.

- When ready to fry, heat the measured oil in the fryer to 325–50°F. Weigh the turkey to calculate the cooking time—the recommended time is 3 to 5 minutes per 1 pound, depending on the size and plumpness of the bird.

- Blot the turkey completely dry with absorbent paper towels, place it on the rack or in the frying basket breast side down and slowly lower it into the hot oil. Fry the turkey for the calculated time and use a meat thermometer or probe to ascertain when the internal temperature reaches 180°F. To do this, lift the turkey out of the fryer and insert the thermometer into the thickest part of the thigh. If the required temperature has not been reached, return the turkey to the oil and continue cooking.

- Once the turkey is done, remove it carefully from the oil and drain it on a platter lined with absorbent paper. Leave it to stand for 15 to 20 minutes before carving to allow the juices to run back into the flesh, making it juicier and easier to carve.

Watchpoints to Deep-fry a Turkey Safely:

- Make sure the fryer is sitting on a completely flat surface with plenty of space around it—fry outdoors for preference, but note that oil dripped on a concrete surface will stain it.

- Wear thick oven mitts to protect your hands.

- Never leave the fryer unattended while the oil is heating or the turkey is cooking.

- Keep children and pets well away from the frying area.

- Keep a fire extinguisher close by.

- Continue to be vigiliant after cooking by leaving the oil to cool down to a safe temperature before you attempt to drain the fryer.

FINAL WATCHPOINTS

- Always protect your hand with an oven mitt when you add food to hot fat.
- Avoid deep-frying large pieces of frozen food. Thaw them thoroughly first and blot with paper towels until completely dry. Small items can be deep-fried from frozen but wipe off any surface moisture and fry at low-moderate temperature 325–50°F so they cook through thoroughly.
- Extra care needs to be taken when deep-frying poultry. Depending on the thickness of the meat, fry at a low-moderate temperature 325°F and test the thickest part of the flesh to see if it is properly cooked with a temperature probe. A large chicken joint or whole bird should never be deep-fried while still frozen. Once immersed in the hot oil, it would cause the oil to boil up and possibly explode.
- Deep-fried food will be very hot straight from the fryer and the denser the food the longer it will retain its heat. When serving deep-fried food as party nibbles, allow items to cool a little before handing around to your guests.
- Anyone with an allergy to peanuts will suffer a similar allergic reaction to food deep-fried in peanut oil.

BELOW Spiced new potatoes are excellent served with curried mayonnaise.

1 | snacks

Every cuisine has its own deep-fried snacks and these recipes are just a few of the well-loved favorites that turn up as street food around the world. Walk down a busy street in cities as diverse as Mumbai, Mexico City, Athens, or Bangkok or stroll through a bustling West Indian market and you'll find it hard to ignore the seductive smells drifting your way from the food stalls set up on every other corner. Crisp pastry parcels with spicy fillings turn up as spring rolls in China and Singapore, as samosas in India, or spanakopittes (phyllo triangles stuffed with spinach and feta cheese) in Greece, while more substantial treats might be Maryland chicken or Louisiana corn dogs. Deep-fried snacks make great party food for all ages and can be served in twists of paper or on paper plates wrapped in mini napkins to save on washing up.

Greek Cheese Pastries

CRISP TRIANGLES OF PHYLLO PASTRY FILLED WITH A TANGY MIX OF CHEESE, EGG, AND HERBS.
WHEN WORKING WITH PHYLLO, USE ONE SHEET AT A TIME AND KEEP THE OTHERS COVERED WITH
PLASTIC WRAP OR A DAMP CLOTH SO THEY DON'T DRY OUT AND BECOME BRITTLE.

MAKES 24

1¾ cups (9 ounces) feta cheese
1 egg, beaten
1 tablespoon chopped fresh
    mint
½ teaspoon dried oregano
½ teaspoon dried thyme
Freshly ground black pepper
8 sheets of phyllo pastry,
    measuring 12 x 7 inches
Oil for deep-frying
Oil or beaten egg for brushing

1 Crumble the feta into a bowl, add the beaten egg, mint, oregano, and thyme and season with freshly ground black pepper. Mash the ingredients together.

2 Unwrap the pastry sheets and place on a board. Brush one sheet lightly with oil and cut lengthways into 3 long strips.

3 Put a teaspoon of the cheese mixture at the corner of one strip. Fold the corner over the filling and keep folding over and over up the strip to make a triangular pastry, pressing the edges together to seal. Repeat until you have made 24 pastries using the remaining filling and phyllo sheets.

4 Heat oil for deep-frying to 350°F and fry the pastries in batches for 2 minutes or until golden brown and crisp. Drain and serve hot or cold.

Corn Dogs

A FAVORITE STREET FOOD SOLD FROM FOOD CARTS ACROSS AMERICA. ALTHOUGH FRANKFURTERS ORIGINATED IN GERMANY, THEY WERE DUBBED "DOGS" IN THE USA AFTER A CARTOON POOCH WITH A SLIMLINE BODY BECAME A CULT FIGURE. IF YOU USE INSTANT OR QUICK-COOK POLENTA FOR MAKING THE BATTER, IT WILL BECOME TOO THICK. IF THIS HAPPENS, SIMPLY STIR IN EXTRA MILK OR WATER.

MAKES 8

1 cup (2 ounces) fine yellow
    cornmeal or polenta
¾ cup (3 ounces) all-purpose
    flour, plus extra for dusting
¼ teaspoon baking soda
¼ teaspoon mild chili powder
⅝ cup (5 fluid ounces)
    buttermilk or thin plain
    yogurt
¼ cup (2 fluid ounces) milk
1 egg
8 frankfurters
Oil for deep-frying

To serve:
Mustard and ketchup

1 Soak 8 wooden skewers in water for 30 minutes so they don't burn in the hot oil.

2 In a bowl, mix together the cornmeal or polenta, flour, baking soda, and chili powder. In another bowl, beat the buttermilk or yogurt, milk, and egg together and pour into the dry ingredients, stirring until smooth.

3 Pat the frankfurters dry with paper towels and dust them with flour. Push a skewer through the length of each, leaving 2 inches sticking out. Heat oil for deep-frying to 350°F.

4 Dip the frankfurters in the batter so they are evenly coated, shaking gently so any excess drips off.

5 Slowly lower four of the frankfurters into the pan—don't drop them in too quickly or they will sink and stick to the basket—and fry for about 4 minutes until golden brown, turning over after 2 minutes. Drain and fry the remaining frankfurters in the same way.

6 Serve the Corn Dogs with mustard and ketchup.

Vegetable Chips ILLUSTRATED RIGHT

PARSNIPS, CARROTS, PLANTAINS, AND SWEET POTATOES CAN ALL BE TURNED INTO VEGETABLE CHIPS TO SERVE WITH DRINKS. IF YOU HAVE A MANDOLINE OR SLICING ATTACHMENT FOR A FOOD PROCESSOR, CUT THE VEGETABLES INTO WAFER-THIN SLICES, IF NOT SHAVE THEM INTO RIBBONS USING A VEGETABLE PEELER.

SERVES 4 TO 6

2 pounds mixed vegetables,
    e.g., parsnips, carrots, sweet
    potatoes
Oil for deep-frying
Salt

1 Peel the vegetables and cut into wafer-thin rounds or ribbons. Pat dry with a paper towel.

2 Heat oil for deep-frying to 350°F and fry the vegetables in batches, without over-crowding the basket. Shake it from time to time so the chips don't stick together.

3 Cook for 3 to 4 minutes or until lightly browned. Drain, cool, and sprinkle with salt before serving.

Hot and Spicy Pasta Crunch

SERVE THIS CRUNCHY, SPICY PASTA WITH PRE-DINNER DRINKS INSTEAD OF NUTS AT A PARTY OR FAMILY GATHERING.

MAKES 9 OUNCES

9 ounces mixed pasta shapes,
    e.g., bows and spirals
1 tablespoon all-purpose flour
2 teaspoons paprika
1 teaspoon hot chili powder
1 teaspoon caraway seeds
Oil for deep-frying
Salt

1 Cook the pasta shapes in a large saucepan of boiling water for 8 to 10 minutes or until tender. Drain and run cold water through the strainer to cool the pasta.

2 Drain thoroughly, transfer the pasta to a bowl and add the flour, paprika, chili powder, and caraway seeds. Toss the shapes until they are all coated in the flour and spices.

3 Heat oil for deep-frying to 350°F and fry the pasta, a little at a time, until slightly golden. Drain off the excess oil on a paper towel.

4 Reheat the oil to 375°F and fry the pasta again in two or three batches until golden brown and crisp. Drain and sprinkle with salt.

Curried Beef Rolls

LARGER VERSIONS OF THESE CRISP PHYLLO ROLLS CAN BE MADE AS A LUNCH OR SUPPER DISH AND SERVED WITH A CRISP MIXED SALAD. WHEN SERVING WITH DRINKS, PILE THE WARM ROLLS ON A PLATTER AND ACCOMPANY WITH A TOMATO DIPPING SAUCE.

MAKES 16

1 shallot
½ red bell pepper
½ green bell pepper
Oil for deep-frying, plus an
    extra 2 tablespoons
8 ounces lean ground beef
1 tablespoon curry paste
2 tablespoons tomato paste
1 cup (8 fluid ounces) beef stock
Salt and pepper
8 sheets phyllo pastry,
    measuring 12 x 7 inches
1 egg, beaten

1 Peel and finely chop the shallot, seed and finely chop the bell peppers.

2 Heat 2 tablespoons of oil in a skillet, add the shallot and bell peppers and fry gently for 5 minutes until softened. Increase the heat under the skillet, add the beef and fry until browned, breaking up any lumps of meat with a spoon.

3 Add the curry paste, tomato paste, and stock, lower the heat and simmer gently with the pan uncovered for 15 minutes until most of the liquid has evaporated and the mixture is quite dry. Season and leave to cool.

4 Cut the phyllo sheets in half across the center to give 16 squares. Brush the edges of one square with beaten egg and spoon a little of the meat mixture in the center. Fold in the sides and roll the phyllo around the filling, sealing tightly. Repeat with the remaining pastry sheets and filling to make 16 rolls.

5 Heat oil for deep-frying to 350°F and fry the rolls in batches for about 3 minutes or until golden and crisp. Drain and serve warm.

Goat Cheese Hashbrowns

THE HASHBROWNS CAN BE COOKED AHEAD AND FROZEN UNTIL NEEDED. TO REHEAT, SPREAD OUT THE STILL-FROZEN HASHBROWN ON A BAKING SHEET AND REHEAT IN A HOT OVEN FOR 10 MINUTES BEFORE ADDING THE TOPPING.

MAKES ABOUT 24

1 pound baking potatoes, e.g., Idaho
4 shallots
2 eggs, beaten
Salt and pepper
Oil for deep-frying
4 ounces soft goat cheese, or another soft cheese
Cherry tomatoes and flat-leaf parsley sprigs, to garnish

1 Peel the potatoes and shred into a bowl. Pour over cold water to cover and set aside for 1 hour. Finely chop the shallots and set aside.

2 Drain the shredded potato and pat dry on a paper towel. Return to the wiped out bowl and mix in the shallots, beaten egg, and seasoning.

3 Heat oil for deep-frying to 350°F and carefully add tablespoons of the potato mixture. Cook in batches for 2 to 3 minutes or until crisp and golden brown. Drain and allow to cool slightly.

4 Spoon a little goat cheese onto each hashbrown, pressing it down lightly, top with cherry tomato quarters and parsley.

Shrimp and Chili Toasts ILLUSTRATED LEFT

THE SHRIMP PASTE CAN BE PREPARED AHEAD AND STORED IN A COVERED BOWL IN THE REFRIGERATOR UNTIL NEEDED BUT THE TOASTS ARE BEST IF COOKED JUST BEFORE SERVING. SERVE WITH PLUM SAUCE OR ANOTHER EAST ASIAN DIP.

MAKES 24

1 pound raw shrimp
4 shallots
1 red chile pepper
1 egg white, lightly beaten
1 teaspoon finely shredded
    fresh ginger
2 teaspoons light soy sauce
1 teaspoon sugar
1 teaspoon sesame oil
Salt and pepper
6 large thin-cut slices of white
    bread, crusts removed
3 tablespoons sesame seeds
Oil for deep-frying

1 Peel, devein, and roughly chop the shrimp. Chop the shallots, seed and chop the red chile pepper.

2 Place the shrimp, shallots, and chile pepper in a food processor or blender and blend to a paste. Transfer to a bowl and stir in the egg white, fresh ginger, soy sauce, sugar, and sesame oil. Season with salt and pepper.

3 Cut each slice of bread into four squares and spread quite thickly with the shrimp paste. Sprinkle the sesame seeds on top.

4 Heat oil for deep-frying to 350°F and fry the toasts three or four at a time, paste-side down, for 2 minutes. Flip them over and fry for a further 2 minutes or until golden brown and crisp.

5 Drain and serve warm with plum sauce or a similar dip.

Fried Bananas in Coconut Batter

A POPULAR STREET SNACK IN THE FAR EAST, PARTICULARLY THAILAND WHERE ROADSIDE CHEFS TOSS THE CRISP BANANA FRITTERS IN WOKS OF CRACKLING OIL. SERVE ON THEIR OWN AS A SNACK OR AS A DESSERT WITH VANILLA ICE CREAM. CHOOSE BANANAS THAT ARE SLIGHTLY UNDER-RIPE SO THEY DON'T BECOME MUSHY WHEN COOKED.

SERVES 4

1 cup (4 ounces) all-purpose flour,
    plus extra to dust
½ teaspoon ground mixed spice
⅓ cup (2 ounces) superfine sugar,
    plus extra to dust
Pinch of salt
1 cup (8 fluid ounces) coconut milk
4 medium, under-ripe bananas
Oil for deep-frying

1 Sift the flour and the mixed spice into a bowl and stir in the sugar and salt. Make a well in the center of the dry ingredients, pour in the coconut milk and mix to a smooth batter. Set aside for 30 minutes.

2 Peel the bananas and cut into ½-inch thick strips, about 3 inches long.

3 Heat oil for deep-frying to 350°F. Dust the banana strips with flour, dip in the batter, and deep-fry in batches for about 2 minutes until golden. Drain and serve dusted with extra superfine sugar.

Maryland Chicken Nuggets with Corn Fritters

FINGER LICKIN' MORSELS OF SUCCULENT CHICKEN WITH THE CLASSIC MARYLAND ACCOMPANIMENTS OF CORN FRITTERS, BACON ROLLS, AND FRIED BANANAS. SERVE AS A SNACK OR IN PAPER CONES AT A PARTY WITH BOWLS OF MUSTARD AND KETCHUP FOR DIPPING.

SERVES 4

2 chicken breasts, skinned and boned
⅔ cup (2 ounces) fresh breadcrumbs
1 tablespoon ground almonds
1 teaspoon dried thyme
¾ cup (3 ounces) all-purpose flour
1 egg, beaten

Corn fritters:
⅔ cup (2 ounces) all-purpose flour
1 egg, beaten
7-ounce can sweetcorn kernels with peppers
2 tablespoons milk

To serve:
2 bananas
4 bacon slices
Oil for deep and shallow frying

1 Cut each chicken breast into four pieces across the grain of the meat. Mix together the breadcrumbs, ground almonds, and thyme and spread out on a plate.

2 Dust the chicken pieces in flour, brush with beaten egg, and coat in the breadcrumb mixture. Chill for 1 hour.

3 To make the fritters, sift the flour into a bowl, add the egg, sweetcorn, and milk and stir until evenly mixed.

4 Peel and cut each banana into four pieces. Halve the bacon slices and roll them up.

5 Heat oil for deep-frying to 350°F and fry the chicken pieces in two batches for 5 minutes until golden brown.

6 Meanwhile, heat oil for shallow frying in a large skillet and drop in tablespoonfuls of the fritter mixture. Fry for 2 minutes on each side until golden. Broil the bacon rolls for 5 minutes until golden brown and crisp.

7 Drain the chicken and fritters and keep warm in a low oven. Dust the banana pieces in flour and fry in the pan used for the fritters until lightly golden. Drain and serve with the chicken, fritters, and bacon rolls.

Spicy Vegetable Rolls with Chili Peanut Dip

IF YOU MAKE THE DIP AHEAD AND IT THICKENS TOO MUCH ON COOLING, STIR IN EXTRA HOT WATER TO BRING IT TO THE RIGHT CONSISTENCY.

MAKES 10

Rolls:

2 small sweet potatoes
1 medium cauliflower
1 leek
4 medium tomatoes
2 tablespoons oil, plus extra for
   deep-frying
1 teaspoon ground turmeric
1 teaspoon ground cumin
2 teaspoons ground coriander
½ cup (2 ounces) frozen peas
10 sheets phyllo pastry,
   measuring 12 x 7 inches

Dip:

1 shallot
1 garlic clove
2 tablespoons oil
4 tablespoons crunchy peanut
   butter
1 tablespoon coconut milk
1 teaspoon hot chili sauce
1 teaspoon brown sugar

1 To make the rolls, peel the sweet potatoes and cut into small dice. Trim the cauliflower and divide into tiny florets. Trim and finely slice the leek. Peel, seed, and dice the tomatoes. Cook the sweet potato and cauliflower in a saucepan of boiling water for 5 minutes or until just tender. Drain.

2 Heat 2 tablespoons of oil in a skillet, add the leek and fry until softened. Sprinkle in the spices and cook for 2 minutes and then add the sweet potato, cauliflower, tomatoes, and frozen peas and fry for 3 minutes. Remove from the heat and leave to cool.

3 Place a sheet of phyllo pastry on a board and spoon a little of the filling down the center. Dampen the edges and roll the phyllo around the filling to enclose, tucking in the sides. Repeat with the remaining phyllo sheets and filling to make 10 rolls.

4 Heat oil for deep-frying to 350°F and fry the rolls in two batches for 4 to 5 minutes or until golden and crisp.

5 While the rolls are cooking, make the dip. Peel and finely chop the shallot and the garlic. Heat the oil in a skillet and gently fry the shallot and the garlic until golden. Stir in the peanut butter, coconut milk, chili sauce, and brown sugar and gradually blend in 1¼ cups (10 fluid ounces) of water. Heat through without boiling. Drain the rolls and serve with the dip.

Fish Sticks

ANY FIRM WHITE FISH COULD BE USED BUT THICKER FILLETS SUCH AS COD OR HADDOCK WORK BETTER THAN FLAT FISH LIKE FLOUNDER OR SOLE. ALLOW THE FISH TO MARINATE FOR ABOUT 20 MINUTES BEFORE FRYING.

SERVES 4

2 garlic cloves
½ teaspoon salt
2 teaspoons shredded fresh
    ginger
Juice of 2 limes
1 pound white fish fillets
All-purpose flour, to dust
1 teaspoon dried thyme
½ teaspoon paprika
1 quantity (about 1½ to 2 cups)
    of Beer Batter No 2 or
    Simple Flour and Water
    Batter (see page 14)
Oil for deep-frying

1 Peel and crush the garlic with the salt. Mix with the shredded ginger and lime juice.

2 Skin the fish, remove any bones and cut into 1-inch sticks across the grain of the flesh.

3 Place the fish in a shallow dish, spread with the garlic and ginger mix and set aside for 20 minutes.

4 Dust the fish sticks with flour. Stir the thyme and paprika into the batter and heat oil for deep-frying to 350°F.

5 Dip the fish in the batter and fry in batches for 2 to 3 minutes until golden brown and crisp. Drain and serve with ketchup or mayonnaise and lemon wedges to squeeze over.

Herby-crumbed Mushrooms with Mustard Mayonnaise ILLUSTRATED RIGHT

TWIST OUT THE MUSHROOM STALKS OR LEAVE THEM IN PLACE, AS YOU PREFER. IF YOU DO REMOVE THEM, THEY CAN BE CHOPPED AND ADDED TO A STOCK, GRAVY, OR SAUCE FOR ANOTHER RECIPE.

SERVES 4

20 medium-sized mushrooms
All-purpose flour, to dust
Salt and pepper
2 eggs, beaten
2 cups (6 ounces) fresh white
    breadcrumbs
1 teaspoon dried thyme
½ teaspoon dried marjoram
Oil for deep-frying
6 tablespoons mayonnaise
2 teaspoons wholegrain
    mustard
Fresh thyme sprigs, to garnish

1 Rinse the mushrooms and pat dry with a paper towel. Dust with seasoned flour and brush with the beaten egg, making sure the gills and stalks are well coated.

2 Mix the breadcrumbs with the thyme and marjoram and press over the mushrooms until evenly covered. Chill for 30 minutes.

3 Heat oil for deep-frying to 350°F and fry the mushrooms in batches for 3 to 4 minutes until golden brown. Drain.

4 Stir the mayonnaise and mustard together and serve with the hot mushrooms. Garnish with fresh thyme sprigs.

Fried Cheese and Ham Sandwiches

INSTEAD OF MOZZARELLA YOU COULD USE EITHER GRUYÈRE OR EMMENTHAL CHEESE TO MAKE THE SANDWICHES AS BOTH CHEESES BECOME DELICIOUSLY CREAMY WHEN COOKED. WHEN COATING THE BREAD IN BEATEN EGG, BRUSH PLENTY DOWN THE SIDES TO MAKE A TIGHT SEAL OR THE CHEESE WILL BUBBLE OUT INTO THE FRYER.

SERVES 4

7 ounces mozzarella
8 large slices of medium-cut
    bread
4 teaspoons smooth mustard
4 thin slices of ham
Oil for deep-frying
2 eggs, beaten

1 Cut the mozzarella into thin slices. Spread the bread with the mustard and cut the slices in half.

2 Sandwich the bread with the mozzarella and ham, making sure none of the cheese slices are poking out the sides of the sandwiches.

3 Heat oil for deep-frying to 350°F. Dip the sandwiches in the beaten egg until well coated and fry in the hot oil for 1 to 2 minutes or until golden brown on both sides. Drain and serve at once with chutney or pickle.

Stamp and Go

THESE JAMAICAN COD CAKES GOT THEIR NAME FROM THE FOOD STALLS WHO USED TO SELL THEM WRAPPED IN PAPER WITH THE WORD "PAID" STAMPED ON THE OUTSIDE—HENCE "STAMP AND GO." IN DAYS GONE BY COD WAS SALTED TO PRESERVE IT BUT, DESPITE THE ADVENT OF REFRIGERATION, "BACALAO," AS SALT COD IS KNOWN IN THE CARIBBEAN ISLANDS, IS STILL POPULAR TODAY.

SERVES 4

9 ounces salt cod
2 garlic cloves
2 bay leaves
1 onion
2 tablespoons oil, plus extra for deep-frying
1 cup (4 ounces) all-purpose flour
1 teaspoon baking powder
1 egg, separated
½ cup (4 fluid ounces) milk
1 tablespoon melted butter
2 tablespoons chopped fresh cilantro
1 tablespoon snipped chives
Pinch of cayenne pepper

1 Soak the salt cod in cold water for 24 hours, changing the water several times. Drain the fish, place in a saucepan and cover with cold water. Peel the garlic cloves and add one to the pan with the bay leaves.

2 Simmer for 15 minutes, then drain the cod and leave to cool. Remove the skin and any bones and flake the flesh.

3 Peel and finely chop the onion. Crush the second clove of garlic. Heat 2 tablespoons of oil in a skillet and fry the onion and garlic until soft and lightly golden.

3 Sift the flour and baking powder into a bowl and beat in the egg yolk, milk, melted butter, cilantro, chives, and cayenne. Add the cod and fried onion and garlic and stir together until well mixed. Leave to stand in the refrigerator for 1 to 2 hours.

4 Whisk the egg white until standing in soft peaks and fold into the cod mixture.

5 Heat oil for deep-frying to 350°F. Using a large spoon, drop small balls of the batter into the oil and fry for 3 to 4 minutes until golden brown. Drain and serve hot.

Tuna Empanadas

IN MEXICO, THESE TORTILLA PARCELS WOULD MOST LIKELY BE STUFFED WITH A SALSA MIXTURE OF SWEETCORN AND MUSHROOMS BUT IN GALICIA IN NORTH-WEST SPAIN, TUNA IS A POPULAR FILLING.

MAKES 12

1 pound fresh tuna steaks
2 medium tomatoes
1 green bell pepper
2 shallots
2 tablespoons olive oil
2 tablespoons chopped fresh
    parsley
4 tablespoons sour cream
12 whole wheat tortillas, about
    6 inches in diameter
1 beaten egg for brushing
Oil for deep-frying

1 Broil the tuna steaks until just cooked, remove any skin and flake the flesh into a bowl.

2 Skin, seed, and finely dice the tomatoes, seed and finely chop the pepper, peel and finely chop the shallots.

3 Heat the olive oil in a saucepan and fry the pepper and shallots until softened. Remove from the heat and stir in the tomatoes, flaked tuna, parsley, and sour cream. Allow to cool.

4 Divide the tuna mix between the tortillas, brush the edges with beaten egg and fold in half to make semi-circular parcels, pressing the edges together to seal.

5 Heat oil for deep-frying to 350°F and fry the empanadas in batches for 3 to 4 minutes until golden and crisp on both sides. Drain and serve warm.

Black-eyed Pea Fritters with Shrimp

THESE SPICY LITTLE FRITTERS ARE FAMILIAR STREET SNACKS IN THE BAHIA REGION OF BRAZIL BUT HAVE THEIR ORIGINS IN AFRICAN SLAVE FOOD. KNOWN AS ACARAJE, THE FRITTERS WOULD BE FRIED IN DENDE (PALM) OIL IN BRAZIL BUT MORE READILY AVAILABLE OILS SUCH AS CORN OR VEGETABLE CAN BE USED INSTEAD. DRIED SHRIMP ARE AVAILABLE FROM ASIAN SUPERMARKETS.

MAKES 16

1¼ cups (8 ounces) dried black-
    eyed peas
1 shallot
½ teaspoon salt
Few drops of chili sauce
2 tablespoons dried shrimp
Oil for deep-frying

To garnish:
16 cooked shrimp
Leaf cilantro sprigs

1 Soak the peas in a bowl of cold water for 24 hours. Drain, then cover with fresh cold water and rub the peas between the palms of your hands to loosen their skins. Leave the skins to float, then skim them off with a slotted spoon and drain the peas thoroughly.

2 Peel and finely chop the shallot. Place in a food processor and add the peas, salt, chili sauce, and dried shrimp. Grind to a soft, smooth puree.

3 Heat oil for deep-frying to 350°F. Drop small spoonfuls of the puree into the oil and fry for 3 to 4 minutes or until golden brown. Serve warm topped with the shrimp and a small sprig of cilantro.

Samosas

THESE VEGETABLE-STUFFED PASTRIES FROM INDIA CAN BE SERVED HOT OR COLD. ACCOMPANY THEM WITH MANGO CHUTNEY OR A DIPPING SAUCE OF THIN PLAIN YOGURT MIXED WITH PLENTY OF CHOPPED FRESH MINT OR A DUST OF PAPRIKA. IN INDIA, COOKS FRY THE SAMOSAS IN GHEE, CLARIFIED BUTTER THAT CAN BE HEATED TO A HIGH TEMPERATURE, BUT OIL CAN ALSO BE USED.

MAKES 16

Pastry:

3 cups (12 ounces) all-purpose flour

Pinch of salt

4 tablespoons oil or ghee, plus extra for shallow and deep-frying

½ cup (4 fluid ounces) generous warm water

Filling:

12 ounces baking potatoes, e.g., Idaho

1 small cauliflower

1½ cups (6 ounces) peas

2 shallots

2 tablespoons curry paste

2 tablespoons chopped fresh cilantro

1 tablespoon lemon juice

Salt and pepper

1 To make the pastry, sift the flour and salt into a bowl. Stir in 4 tablespoons of oil or ghee, and add 6 to 7 tablespoons of cold water. Mix to a dough.

2 Knead the dough on a floured board until smooth, wrap in plastic wrap, and leave to rest for about 30 minutes.

3 To make the filling, scrub the potatoes and, without peeling, cook them in a saucepan of boiling water until tender. Drain and when cool, peel and chop into small dice.

4 Divide the cauliflower into tiny florets and blanch in a saucepan of boiling water for 2 to 3 minutes or until just tender, then drain. If using fresh peas, blanch them with the cauliflower, if using frozen they need no pre-cooking.

5 Peel and slice the shallots. Heat 3 tablespoons of oil in a large skillet and fry the shallots until soft. Add the potatoes, cauliflower, peas, curry paste, cilantro, and lemon juice and cook over a low heat for 2 to 3 minutes, stirring frequently. Set aside to cool.

6 Divide the pastry into 8 and, keeping the pieces you are not working with covered, roll one piece to a 7-inch round. Cut in half and shape each semi-circle into a cone, dampening the edges to seal. Spoon in a little of the filling, dampen the top, and press down over the filling to enclose it. Use the remaining pastry and filling to make 16 samosas.

7 Heat oil for deep-frying to 350°F and fry the samosas in batches for 3 to 4 minutes until golden brown on both sides. Drain and serve hot or cold.

Sesame Turkey Bites

THESE ARE GOOD SERVED WITH A CREAMY TOMATO AND RED BELL PEPPER DIP, TOMATO SALSA, OR AVOCADO AND BLUE CHEESE DIP (SEE PAGE 52). THEY CAN BE SERVED HOT OR COLD.

MAKES ABOUT 30

Turkey Bites:
1 pound ground raw turkey breast
1 tablespoon snipped fresh chives
2 teaspoons wholegrain mustard
Salt and pepper
4 tablespoons white sesame seeds
1 teaspoon black sesame seeds
Oil for deep-frying

Dip:
½ red bell pepper
6 tablespoons ricotta
2 tablespoons ketchup
Dash of Tabasco sauce
2 teaspoons snipped fresh chives

To serve:
15 cherry tomatoes, halved
Cucumber slices

1 To make the turkey bites, mix together the ground turkey, chives, mustard, and seasoning in a bowl. Roll the mixture into about 30 walnut-sized balls.

2 Mix the white and black sesame seeds together and roll the turkey balls in the seeds until coated. Chill for 30 minutes or longer.

3 Heat oil for deep-frying to 325°F and fry the turkey balls in batches for 3 to 4 minutes until golden.

4 To make the dip, finely chop the pepper. Mix together the ricotta, ketchup, and Tabasco sauce until smooth. Stir in the pepper and sprinkle with the chives.

5 Drain the turkey balls and skewer on cocktail sticks with half a cherry tomato and some cucumber slices. Serve with the dip.

Pork and Shrimp Wontons

SERVE THESE CRISP LITTLE "MONEYBAGS" WITH AN ASIAN DIPPING SAUCE SUCH AS CHILI, SWEET AND SOUR, PLUM, OR DARK SOY. WONTON WRAPPERS ARE AVAILABLE IN PACKS FROM THE FROZEN SECTION OF CHINESE SUPERMARKETS.

MAKES 20

5 ounces raw shrimp

3 canned water chestnuts

2 scallions

7 ounces lean ground pork

1 teaspoon fresh ginger, finely
   shredded

2 tablespoons light soy sauce

1 tablespoon oyster sauce

1 tablespoon fish sauce

20 wonton wrappers

1 egg white, lightly beaten

Oil for deep-frying

1 Peel and devein the shrimp and chop finely. Finely chop the water chestnuts and scallions. Put the pork, ginger, shrimp, water chestnuts, soy, oyster, and fish sauces, and scallions in a bowl and stir until well mixed.

2 Place a teaspoon of the mixture in the center of a wonton wrapper, brush the edges of the wrapper with egg white and gather it around the filling, pressing the edges together at the top to make a "money bag" shape. As you make them, place the filled wontons on a floured board, spaced slightly apart, so they don't stick to the board or each other.

3 Heat oil for deep-frying to 325°F and cook in batches for 3 minutes or until golden and crisp.

4 Drain the wontons and serve hot with the dipping sauce.

Spicy Thai Fish Cakes with Cilantro Soy Dip

THESE CAN ALSO BE SERVED AS AN APPETIZER WITH A SMALL SALAD GARNISH AND THE DIPPING SAUCE SPOONED OVER. A MIXTURE OF SALMON AND A FIRM WHITE FISH SUCH AS COD IS USED HERE BUT YOU COULD JUST USE SALMON IF YOU PREFER.

MAKES 20

8 ounces salmon fillet, skinned

8 ounces firm white fish fillet, e.g., cod

4 ounces fine green beans

1 teaspoon fresh lemon grass puree

1 teaspoon fresh ginger puree

Rind of 1 lime, finely shredded

1 tablespoon fish sauce

1 tablespoon chopped fresh cilantro

1 egg white, lightly beaten

All-purpose flour, to dust

Oil for deep-frying

Dip:

1 tablespoon coriander seeds

4 tablespoons dark soy sauce

1 tablespoon white wine vinegar

½ teaspoon granulated sugar

A few fresh cilantro leaves, chopped

1 Cut the salmon and white fish into chunks. Trim and finely chop the green beans.

2 Place the salmon, white fish, lemon grass puree, ginger puree, and lime rind in a food processor and blend until coarsely ground—be careful not to reduce the mixture to a paste. Transfer to a bowl and stir in the fish sauce, cilantro, green beans, and egg white.

3 With floured hands, shape into small balls and flatten into round cakes, about ½-inch thick. Chill for 30 minutes.

4 To make the dip, toast the coriander seeds in a dry, heavy-bottomed skillet until golden. Remove from the pan and mix with the soy sauce, vinegar, and sugar, stirring until the sugar dissolves. Pour into a serving bowl and float a few fresh cilantro leaves on top.

5 Heat oil for deep-frying to 325°F. Dust the fish cakes in flour and fry in batches for 2 to 3 minutes until golden. Drain and serve with the dipping sauce.

Fried Cheese with Cranberry and Olive Relish ILLUSTRATED LEFT

USE SMALL, INDIVIDUAL PORTIONS OF CAMEMBERT OR WEDGES OF BRIE CUT FROM A LARGE CHEESE. WHICHEVER YOU USE, THE CHEESE SHOULD BE QUITE FIRM SO IT DOESN'T MELT IN THE HOT OIL.

SERVES 4

3 tablespoons all-purpose flour
1 egg
¾ cup (3 ounces) dry breadcrumbs
8 small wedges of Camembert or Brie
Oil for deep-frying
4 tablespoons cranberry sauce
1 tablespoon chopped pitted olives
Salad, to garnish

1 Spread out the flour on a plate, beat the egg in a shallow dish, and spoon the breadcrumbs on to another plate.

2 Dust the cheese wedges with flour, dip in the beaten egg and then press on the crumbs until well coated. Chill for 30 minutes.

3 Heat oil for deep-frying to 350°F and fry the cheeses in two batches for about 1 to 2 minutes each or until golden. Drain on paper towels.

4 Warm the cranberry sauce with the olives. Stir well and serve with the hot cheese and a salad garnish.

Spinach and Feta Cigars

IF USING FROZEN SPINACH, THAW IT COMPLETELY AND THEN DRY IT OFF IN A DRY, HEAVY-BOTTOMED SKILLET OVER A LOW HEAT UNTIL ALL THE EXCESS MOISTURE HAS EVAPORATED.

MAKES 20

3 ounces feta cheese
8 ounces cooked spinach
¼ cup (2 ounces) cottage cheese
1 teaspoon chopped fresh mint
Pinch of ground nutmeg
10 sheets phyllo pastry, measuring 7 x 12 inches
1 egg white, lightly beaten
Oil for deep-frying

1 Crumble the feta cheese and chop the spinach. In a bowl, mix together the spinach, cottage cheese, feta, mint, and nutmeg, stirring until evenly combined.

2 Cut the phyllo sheets in half to give 20 squares. Spoon a little of the spinach mixture down the center of one square, brush the edges with egg white and roll up the pastry around the filling in a cigar shape, pressing the edges together to seal.

3 Repeat with the rest of the phyllo squares and the filling to make 20 cigars.

4 Heat oil for deep-frying to 350°F and fry the cigars in batches for 2 to 3 minutes or until golden brown. Drain and serve warm.

Cheese Aigrettes with Chili Tomato Sauce

ADD A STRONGLY FLAVORED HARD CHEESE, SUCH AS PARMESAN, TO THE AIGRETTES AND VARY THE AMOUNT OF CHILI IN THE SAUCE ACCORDING TO PERSONAL TASTE.

SERVES 4

Tomato sauce:

4 medium ripe tomatoes
2 shallots
1 small red chile
2 tablespoons olive oil
1 teaspoon dried oregano
1 teaspoon granulated sugar

Aigrettes:

⅝ cup (5 fluid ounces) cold
    water
2 ounces (½ stick) butter
½ cup (2½ ounces) all-purpose
    flour
2 eggs, beaten
2 tablespoons shredded hard
    cheese, e.g., Parmesan
    cheese
1 teaspoon mustard powder
Oil for deep-frying
Extra finely shredded Parmesan
    cheese, to dust

1 To make the tomato sauce, peel, seed, and chop the tomatoes. Peel and finely chop the shallots, seed and finely chop the chile.

2 Heat the olive oil in a saucepan, add the shallots and fry until softened. Add the chile, tomatoes, oregano, and sugar and simmer uncovered for 15 to 20 minutes so the excess liquid in the tomatoes evaporates and you have a thick sauce—mash the tomatoes occasionally so they break down.

3 To make the aigrettes, put the water in a saucepan, cut the butter into small pieces and add. Heat until the butter melts, then bring to a fast boil. Remove from the heat and add all the flour in one go. Beat with a wooden spoon until you have a smooth mixture that leaves the sides of the pan.

4 Gradually beat in the eggs until the paste is soft and glossy but still holds its shape. Finally beat in the cheese and mustard powder.

5 Heat oil for deep-frying to 350°F. Drop large spoonfuls of the mixture into the hot oil and fry for 5 minutes or until golden brown all over. Drain, dust with extra Parmesan, and serve at once with the warm sauce.

2 | appetizers

Serving an appetizer that complements the dishes to follow, is one of the secrets of

a successful dinner party. If your main course is rich and full flavored, opt for a

simple appetizer that's not too filling, if the main course is a lighter dish of chicken

or fish, the appetizer can be more substantial. While delicious to eat, some deep-

fried foods can look dull if served on their own, so add a dusting

of paprika or finely shredded cheese, a

few scattered chives, a lettuce leaf

and cherry tomato, or a fresh

herb sprig for a

colorful garnish.

Chinese Aromatic and Crispy Duck

SIMILAR TO THE WORLD-FAMOUS PEKING DUCK BUT SIMPLER TO PREPARE. IT MAKES AN EXCELLENT STARTER FOR A CHINESE DINNER PARTY BUT COULD ALSO BE SERVED AS A MAIN COURSE FOR 2 TO 3 PEOPLE. AS THE DUCK HAS TO STEAM FOR SEVERAL HOURS AND THEN BE LEFT TO COOL, IT IS WORTH DOING THE INITIAL COOKING THE DAY BEFORE YOU PLAN TO SERVE IT.

SERVES 4 TO 6

1 plump duck, weighing about
    3½ pounds

Marinade:
6 tablespoons light soy sauce
2 tablespoons rice wine or dry
    sherry
2 teaspoons Chinese five spice
    powder
2 teaspoons shredded fresh
    ginger
Oil for deep-frying

To serve:
Thin Chinese pancakes
Plum dipping sauce
Shredded shallots
Cucumber spears

1 Remove the wing tips from the duck and split it in half lengthways (or ask the butcher to do this for you). Rinse the duck halves and pat dry with absorbent paper towels.

2 To make the marinade, whisk together the soy sauce, rice wine or sherry, Chinese five spice powder, and ginger in a shallow dish large enough to take both halves of the duck. Place the duck in the dish and baste it with the marinade. Cover and leave in a cool place for 3 to 4 hours, turning over the duck from time to time.

3 Transfer the duck to a steamer (add any remaining marinade to the steaming water) and steam for 3 hours, topping up the water as necessary.

4 Remove the duck from the steamer and leave overnight in a cool, dry place. It is important for the duck skin to be dry or it will not crisp when fried.

5 Heat oil for deep-frying to 350°F and deep-fry the duck halves, skin side down, for 5 to 6 minutes or until deep golden brown and crisp. Drain the duck and shred the meat and skin into small pieces.

6 To serve, spread the pancakes with plum sauce and top with pieces of duck, shredded shallots, and cucumber spears, roll up and eat.

Pumpkin Puffs with Avocado and Blue Cheese Dip

IF MAKING THE DIP MORE THAN 1 HOUR BEFORE SERVING, PRESS A PIECE OF PLASTIC WRAP OVER THE SURFACE TO EXCLUDE THE AIR AND PREVENT THE AVOCADO TURNING BROWN.

SERVES 4

1 pound pumpkin (peeled and
    seeded weight)
4 scallions
1 tablespoon butter
Salt and pepper
1 egg, beaten
2 tablespoons all-purpose flour
Oil for deep-frying

Avocado and blue cheese dip:
1 ripe avocado
1 tablespoon lemon juice
½ cup (2 ounces) crumbled blue
    cheese
½ cup (4 fluid ounces) Greek-
    style plain yogurt
Few drops of Tabasco sauce

1 Cut the pumpkin into chunks and steam for 10 minutes or until tender. Drain and mash. Finely chop the scallions and stir into the mashed pumpkin with the butter, seasoning, beaten egg, and flour.

2 Heat oil for deep-frying to 350°F. Using a large spoon, drop spoonfuls of the pumpkin mix into the hot oil and fry in batches for 3 to 4 minutes until golden brown.

3 To make the dip, peel and mash the avocado with the lemon juice. Mix in the blue cheese, yogurt, and Tabasco sauce to taste. Alternatively, the ingredients can be blended together in a food processor or blender.

4 Serve the hot fritters with the dip.

Walnut Chicken

SERVE AS A DINNER PARTY APPETIZER WITH THE CILANTRO AND CARROT PUREE OR AS PART OF A FINGER FOOD BUFFET WITH A LEMON OR CURRY MAYONNAISE DIP.

SERVES 6

4 chicken breasts, skinned and
    boned
Juice of 1 lemon
1 teaspoon shredded fresh
    ginger
All-purpose flour, to dust
1 egg, beaten
1 cup (5 ounces) walnuts, finely
    chopped
Oil for deep-frying

Cilantro and carrot puree:
1 pound carrots
1¼ cups chicken stock
2 tablespoons chopped fresh
    cilantro

1 Cut each chicken breast across into 4 or 5 strips. Spread out in a shallow dish and add the lemon juice and ginger. Allow to marinate for several hours, turning the chicken occasionally.

2 Lift the chicken pieces from the marinade and pat dry with paper towels. Dust them with the flour, brush with beaten egg, and press on the chopped walnuts until evenly coated. Chill for 30 minutes or until ready to cook.

3 Heat oil for deep-frying to 350°F and fry the chicken in batches for 3 to 4 minutes until cooked through and the coating is a rich golden brown.

4 To make the puree, peel and chop the carrots and simmer in the stock in a covered saucepan for 10 minutes or until tender. Blend the carrots and cooking liquid and stir in the cilantro. Serve warm with the chicken.

Suppli di Riso

CRISP-COATED BALLS OF RISOTTO RICE ARE POPULAR ALL OVER ITALY AND ARE MADE WITH A VARIETY OF FILLINGS INCLUDING MEAT, CHEESE, OR VEGETABLES.

SERVES 4

1 cup risotto (arborio) rice
Salt and pepper
1 egg, beaten
5 ounces mozzarella cheese
1 cup (5 ounces) dry
    breadcrumbs
½ teaspoon dried marjoram
Oil for deep-frying

To serve:
Chunky tomato pasta sauce

1 Cook the rice in a saucepan of boiling water for 12 to 15 minutes until just tender, or according to the packet instructions. Drain and leave to cool. Then, season the rice with salt and pepper and stir in the beaten egg.

2 Cut the mozzarella into 12 cubes. Place a tablespoon of cooked rice in one hand, add a cube of cheese and cover the cheese with more rice. Mold the rice around the cheese and press into a ball. Repeat with the remaining rice and cheese.

3 Mix together the breadcrumbs and marjoram. Roll the rice balls in the crumb mixture until coated. Chill for 2 to 3 hours.

4 Heat oil for deep-frying to 375°F. Fry the balls in 2 or 3 batches for 3 to 4 minutes until golden. Drain and serve hot with chunky tomato pasta sauce.

Lobster and Avocado Cups

EITHER CHINESE SPRING ROLL WRAPPERS OR PHYLLO PASTRY CAN BE USED TO MAKE THE "CUPS" AND CUT THE SHEETS TO THE CORRECT SIZE WITH SCISSORS IF NECESSARY. FOR CONVENIENCE, THE CUPS CAN BE PREPARED AND FRIED SEVERAL HOURS AHEAD AND LARGE SHRIMP, CRAWFISH, OR A MIX OF DIFFERENT SEAFOOD CAN REPLACE THE LOBSTER IN THE FILLING.

SERVES 4

12 squares of phyllo pastry or
    spring roll wrappers,
    roughly 7 inches in size
Oil for deep-frying
1 pound cooked lobster meat
1 avocado
Juice of 1 lime
4 cherry tomatoes
¼ cucumber
½ bag of mixed lettuce leaves
4 tablespoons seafood or
    Thousand Island dressing
4 teaspoons lumpfish caviar or
    salmon roe

1 Layer up the phyllo squares or spring roll wrappers in stacks of three, dampening each sheet to help the layers stick together and positioning the corners at different angles. Cover with a sheet of plastic wrap and a damp cloth to prevent the pastry drying out.

2 Heat oil for deep-frying to 350°F. Carefully add one stack of pastry to the oil, place a ladle in the center and press down into a cup shape. Fry for 3 to 4 minutes until golden brown, using the ladle to ensure the pastry "cup" keeps its shape and stays immersed in the oil but avoid pressing down too firmly or the pastry will stick firmly to the ladle, making it difficult to remove without breaking.

3 Remove from the oil and gently loosen the cup from the ladle.

4 Cut the lobster meat into bite-sized pieces. Peel and slice the avocado and toss with the lime juice. Halve the cherry tomatoes and slice the cucumber.

5 Place the cups on serving plates and line with lettuce leaves. Fill with the lobster, avocado, tomatoes, and cucumber. Spoon on the dressing and roe.

Shrimp Wraps with a Lemon Grass Dip

IT'S IMPORTANT TO USE GREEN (RAW) SHRIMP AS PRE-COOKED ONES WILL OVERCOOK IN THE HOT OIL AND LOSE THEIR FLAVOR AND SUCCULENCE.

SERVES 4

Dip:

1 stick of lemon grass or
1 teaspoon lemon grass
puree
1 red chile pepper
1 teaspoon light brown sugar
4 tablespoons soy sauce
1 tablespoon rice vinegar
1 tablespoon chopped fresh
cilantro

Shrimp:

12 large green shrimp
12 pieces of phyllo pastry or
Chinese spring roll
wrappers, each measuring
7 x 3 inches
1 egg, beaten
Oil for deep-frying

1 For the dip, if using a stick of lemon grass, chop into very fine pieces. Seed and finely chop the chile pepper. Mix together the lemon grass, chile pepper, sugar, soy sauce, and rice vinegar and set aside for 1 hour for the flavors to infuse. When ready to serve, pour into a bowl or divide between four small dishes and scatter over the fresh cilantro.

2 For the shrimp, peel off the shells and remove the heads but leave the tails on. Slit down the back of each shrimp and pull out the black thread running down it. Rinse the shrimp and pat dry with a paper towel.

3 Place one piece of phyllo or spring roll wrapper on a board. Brush the edges with beaten egg. Place a shrimp at one end and roll the wrapper around it, leaving the shrimp tail exposed. Press the wrapper edges together to seal. Repeat with the remaining shrimp and wrappers.

4 Put the wrapped shrimp side-by-side on a plate and chill until ready to cook. Heat oil for deep-frying to 350°F and fry the shrimp in batches for 2 minutes or until golden brown.

5 Drain and serve hot with the dip.

Miso Soup with Fried Bean Curd

DASHI IS A LIGHT STOCK WIDELY USED IN JAPANESE CUISINE. PACKS OF READY-MADE DASHI ARE AVAILABLE FROM JAPANESE FOOD STORES BUT DETAILS OF HOW TO PREPARE IT ARE GIVEN HERE IF YOU PREFER TO MAKE YOUR OWN. KELP, BONITO FLAKES, AND MISO CAN ALSO BE FOUND IN JAPANESE SUPERMARKETS.

SERVES 4

Dashi stock:
½–inch strip of dried kelp
4¼ cups (18 fluid ounces) water
2 tablespoons dried bonito
    flakes

Other ingredients:
3 ounces shiitake mushrooms
½ red bell pepper
7 ounces firm tofu (beancurd)
2 ounces snow peas
2 ounces brown or red miso
All-purpose flour, to dust
Oil for deep-frying

1 Wipe the kelp with a damp cloth and cut into three or four pieces. Place the pieces in a large saucepan with the water and bring slowly to a boil. As the water comes up to a boil, remove the kelp with a draining spoon and discard.

2 Sprinkle in the bonito flakes and remove the pan from the heat. As soon as the flakes start to sink, strain the stock through a fine strainer and discard the flakes.

3 When ready to make the soup, slice the mushrooms and the pepper, cut the tofu into small cubes, and slice the snow peas.

4 Heat the dashi stock in a saucepan until simmering. Add the miso and stir until dissolved. Add the mushrooms and snow peas and leave the soup over a low heat, without letting it boil, while you cook the tofu.

5 Dust the cubes of tofu with flour and heat oil for deep-frying to 350°F. Fry the tofu for 1 to 2 minutes until golden, drain, and divide between four bowls. Ladle the soup into the bowls and serve at once.

Salmon Beignets with Creamy Fennel Sauce

FENNEL'S MILD ANISEED FLAVOR GOES VERY WELL WITH FISH AND THESE LIGHT, CRISP BEIGNETS MAKE A DELICIOUS APPETIZER. THEY COULD ALSO BE SERVED AS A STYLISH SUPPER DISH, WASHED DOWN WITH A CRISP GLASS OF CALIFORNIAN CHARDONNAY.

SERVES 6

6 tablespoons (3 ounces) butter
⅔ cup (6 fluid ounces) water
⅜ cup (3 fluid ounces) milk
1 cup (4 ounces) strong all-
    purpose flour
3 medium eggs, beaten
5 ounces hot smoked salmon
2 tablespoons finely shredded
    Parmesan
½ teaspoon paprika
1 tablespoon lemon juice
Salt and pepper
Oil for deep-frying

Sauce:
6 tablespoons lemon mayonnaise
4 tablespoons sour cream
1 tablespoon finely chopped
    fresh fennel sprigs

1 Cut up the butter into small pieces and place in a saucepan with the water and milk. Heat until the butter melts, bring to a rolling boil and add the flour in one go. Beat with a wooden spoon until the mixture forms a smooth ball.

2 Allow to cool slightly, then beat in the eggs a little at a time until you have a soft mixture that holds its shape.

3 Remove any skin and bones from the salmon and flake the flesh. Stir into the batter with the Parmesan, paprika, lemon juice, and seasoning.

4 Heat oil for deep-frying to 325°F and drop in walnut-sized balls of the mixture. Fry in batches for 5 to 6 minutes or until golden.

5 To make the sauce, stir the mayonnaise, sour cream, and fennel together until combined. Drain the beignets and serve hot with the sauce.

Crisp-fried Avocado Rings with Shrimp Sauce

A VARIATION ON THE TRADITIONAL AVOCADO WITH SHRIMP, THIS MAKES AN UNUSUAL DINNER PARTY APPETIZER. IT'S IMPORTANT THE AVOCADOS ARE RIPE BUT IF THEY ARE OVER-RIPE THEY WILL BE DIFFICULT TO COAT WITH THE CRUMBS. THE RINGS SHOULD BE FRIED WITHIN 30 MINUTES OF COATING THEM TO AVOID DISCOLORATION.

SERVES 4

1 cup (3 ounces) fresh
    breadcrumbs, white or
    brown
1 tablespoon ground hazelnuts
2 large avocados
All-purpose flour, to dust
1 egg, beaten
Oil for deep-frying

Sauce:
4 ounces peeled shrimp
2 tablespoons mayonnaise
4 tablespoons light cream
2 teaspoons ketchup
Juice of 1 lime

To garnish:
4 whole shrimp
4 lime wedges
2 tablespoons chopped parsley
¼ teaspoon paprika

1 Mix together the breadcrumbs and hazelnuts and spread out on a plate.

2 Cut the unpeeled avocados into rings about ¼-inch thick using a small sharp knife and gently ease the rings off the pits. Peel away the skin from the rings, dip them in flour, brush with beaten egg, and coat with the crumb mixture.

3 Heat about 1 inch oil in a large skillet to 350°F and fry the avocado rings for 2 to 3 minutes until golden, turning over after 1 minute. Drain.

4 To make the sauce, coarsely chop the shrimp and mix with the mayonnaise, light cream, ketchup, and lime juice. Serve with the warm avocado rings and garnish with whole shrimp, lime wedges, chopped parsley, and a sprinkling of paprika.

Halloumi and Zucchini Fritters

HALLOUMI IS A FIRM, WHITE CHEESE FROM CYPRUS AND HAS A TANGY, SALTY TASTE. IT CAN BE FOUND IN LARGER SUPERMARKETS AND GREEK FOOD STORES.

SERVES 4

5 ounces halloumi cheese
4 ounces feta cheese
1 zucchini
¾ cup (3 ounces) all-purpose
    flour
2 tablespoons milk
1 egg
2 tablespoons chopped fresh
    cilantro or parsley
Oil for deep-frying
4 tablespoons Greek yogurt
½ teaspoon paprika

1 Cut the halloumi cheese into fine dice, crumble the feta, and shred the zucchini.

2 In a bowl, mix together the halloumi, feta, zucchini, and flour. Whisk together the milk and egg and stir into the cheese mixture with half the cilantro or parsley to make a thick batter.

3 Heat oil for deep-frying to 350°F. Using a large spoon, drop three spoonfuls of the mixture into the oil and fry for 30 seconds on each side or until golden brown.

4 Drain and fry the remaining mixture in the same way to make 12 fritters.

5 Divide the warm fritters between serving plates and spoon the Greek yogurt alongside. Dust with the paprika and scatter over the remaining cilantro or parsley.

Cauliflower Cheese Bites

SERVE AS AN APPETIZER WITH A SPOONFUL OF THOUSAND ISLAND DRESSING AND A SMALL SALAD GARNISH, OR AS A VEGETABLE ACCOMPANIMENT TO SAUSAGES, BURGERS, OR PLAINLY BROILED MEAT.

SERVES 4

1 medium size cauliflower
1 cup (4 ounces) all-purpose
    flour
Pinch of mustard powder
Salt and pepper
2 eggs, separated
¾ cup (3 ounces) shredded
    Cheddar cheese
2 tablespoons oil, plus extra for
    deep-frying
½ cup (4 fluid ounces) water
All-purpose flour, to dust

1 Divide the cauliflower into small florets, discarding the tough center stalk. Cook the florets in a saucepan of boiling water for about 5 minutes or until just tender. Drain.

2 Sift the flour and mustard into a bowl and season with pepper. Stir in the egg yolks, cheese, 2 tablespoons of oil, and the water, whisking until you have a smooth batter.

3 Heat oil for deep-frying to 375°F. While the oil is heating up, whisk the egg whites until stiff and fold into the batter.

4 Dust the cauliflower florets with flour and dip them into the batter until they are well coated. Deep-fry for about 4 minutes until golden brown, drain and serve at once.

3 | meat & poultry

The Chinese are famous for their deep-fried meat dishes such as Sweet and Sour

Pork and Lemon Chicken, while the Ukraine introduced gourmets to Chicken Kiev,

but it is the United States that has turned its Southern Fried Chicken into one of the

world's most popular fast foods. These

are just a few of the tasty fried foods

featured in this chapter.

Southern Fried Chicken with Cream Gravy

THERE ARE ALMOST AS MANY WAYS OF COOKING THIS FAMOUS DISH AS THERE ARE SOUTHERN STATES, ONE OF THE MOST POPULAR COMING FROM MARYLAND (SEE PAGE 30), BUT THIS VERSION COATS THE CHICKEN IN A MIX OF HERBS AND CAJUN SPICES.

SERVES 4

8 chicken joints, a mix of
    drumsticks and thighs
2 cups (8 ounces) all-purpose
    flour
Salt and pepper
1 teaspoon mixed dried herbs
1 teaspoon Cajun seasoning
1 teaspoon granulated sugar
Oil for deep-frying

Cream gravy:
2 tablespoons all-purpose flour
1 cup (8 fluid ounces) whole
    milk

1 Rinse the chicken joints and pat dry with paper towels.

2 Put the flour, salt, pepper, herbs, Cajun seasoning, and granulated sugar in a plastic food bag, seal the top and shake well to combine. Add the chicken pieces, two at a time, and toss to coat with the flour mixture. Place the coated chicken pieces on a plate and chill for 30 minutes.

3 Heat oil for deep-frying to 325°F and fry the chicken for about 15 minutes until golden brown. Drain and test the chicken is cooked through, either by cutting into the flesh with a sharp knife or by using a meat temperature probe.

4 To make the cream gravy, spoon 2 tablespoons of the frying oil into a saucepan and stir in the flour. Cook for 1 minute, then remove from the heat and gradually mix in the milk. Return to a low heat and stir until thickened and smooth.

5 Serve the chicken with the gravy and with vegetables of your choice.

Gingered Lemon Chicken

A CANTONESE DISH FROM HONG KONG THAT CAN BE SERVED WITH FRIED RICE, PLAIN BOILED RICE, OR EGG NOODLES. AS THE VEGETABLES ARE STIR-FRIED FIRST, BEFORE EXTRA OIL IS ADDED TO DEEP-FRY THE CHICKEN, A WOK IS THE MOST PRACTICAL PAN TO USE.

SERVES 4

1 quantity (about 1½ to 2 cups) of Simple Flour and Water Batter (see page 14)
1 red bell pepper
1 zucchini
4 scallions
4 boneless chicken breasts, skinned
2 tablespoons oil, plus extra for deep-frying
All-purpose flour, for dusting

Lemon sauce:
1½ tablespoons cornstarch
½ cup (4 fluid ounces) freshly-squeezed lemon juice
1½ cups (12 fluid ounces) chicken stock
2 tablespoons clear honey
2 tablespoons light brown sugar
1 tablespoon shredded fresh ginger

1 Make up the batter and leave to stand for at least 30 minutes.

2 Seed and chop the pepper, slice or chop the zucchini, and chop the scallions. Cut each chicken breast into 3 pieces.

3 Heat 2 tablespoons of oil in a wok and stir-fry the pepper, zucchini, and scallions for 3 to 4 minutes until starting to soften. Remove from the wok and keep warm in a low oven.

4 Add extra oil to the wok to deep-fry the chicken and heat to 350°F. Dip the chicken pieces in flour and then in the batter and deep-fry for 8 to 10 minutes until golden.

5 For the sauce, whisk the cornstarch and lemon juice together until smooth. Pour into a saucepan and stir in the stock, honey, sugar, and ginger. Stir over a low heat until the sauce comes to a boil and it clears and thickens. Simmer for 1 minute.

6 Drain the chicken and serve with the vegetables with the lemon sauce spooned over.

Rice Vermicelli with Chicken and Shrimp

IN THE FAR EAST, COOKS USE WOKS FOR DEEP-FRYING AS WELL AS STIR-FRYING AND THIS RECIPE IS A COMBINATION OF BOTH COOKING METHODS.

SERVES 4

1 tablespoon lime juice
1 teaspoon crushed garlic
1 tablespoon brown sugar
3 tablespoons light soy sauce
1 tablespoon rice vinegar
9 ounces boneless chicken breasts
1 carrot
1 red bell pepper
1 small zucchini
7 ounces rice vermicelli
Oil for deep-frying
6 ounces peeled shrimp
2 eggs, beaten
2 tablespoons chopped fresh cilantro

1 Whisk together the lime juice, garlic, sugar, soy sauce, and vinegar. Set to one side.

2 Skin the chicken breasts and cut the flesh into thin strips. Peel and cut the carrot into matchsticks, seed and chop the pepper, and cut the zucchini into matchsticks.

3 Snip the dry vermicelli into short lengths and soak in warm water for a few minutes until softened. Spread out on a tray and leave until dry.

4 Heat oil for deep-frying in a wok to 375°F and fry the vermicelli in batches until light golden and crisp. Drain and set aside.

5 Pour off most of the oil from the wok, leaving about 2 tablespoons. Reheat, add the chicken, and stir-fry for 3 minutes. Remove and set aside. Add the carrot, pepper, and zucchini and stir-fry for 3 minutes.

6 Return the chicken to the wok, add the shrimp, and pour in the soy sauce mixture. Toss over the heat for 1 to 2 minutes, add the beaten eggs, and stir until they have set. Add the vermicelli and toss together until well mixed.

7 Serve at once before the noodles have started to soften, with the cilantro sprinkled over.

Chicken Kiev

IN THIS RECIPE IT IS ESSENTIAL THE OIL IS HEATED TO THE CORRECT TEMPERATURE. IF IT IS TOO HOT, THE CRUMB COATING WILL BROWN TOO QUICKLY BEFORE THE CHICKEN INSIDE IS COOKED. SHOULD THIS HAPPEN, DRAIN THE CHICKEN JOINTS, PLACE THEM ON A BAKING SHEET AND FINISH COOKING IN A 350°F OVEN FOR 10 TO 15 MINUTES.

SERVES 4

4 large garlic cloves

Salt and pepper

4 tablespoons chopped fresh
   parsley

6 tablespoons (3 ounces) butter,
   at room temperature

1 teaspoon lemon juice

Four 8-ounce chicken supremes
   (breasts with wing bones
   attached, skinned)

All-purpose flour, to dust

3 eggs, beaten

2 cups (8 ounces) dry
   breadcrumbs

Light olive oil for deep-frying

1 Crush the garlic on a board with a little salt and mix with the parsley. Work in the butter and lemon juice and season with pepper. Spoon the mixture on to a sheet of plastic wrap and shape into a log roughly ½–inch thick. Wrap the plastic around the butter and twist the ends in a tight parcel. Chill or freeze until firm.

2 Place each supreme between two sheets of plastic wrap and beat with a rolling pin or the flat side of a meat mallet, avoiding the wing bone. The supremes should be beaten out to roughly double their size and the thinner the edges are, the better the "seal" will be.

3 Unwrap the garlic butter and cut into four sticks. Open up the breast part of each supreme and place a butter stick in the center. Wrap the flesh around the butter, tucking in the sides to enclose it completely.

4 Dust each supreme with flour, brush with beaten egg, and coat in breadcrumbs. Chill for 1 hour and then coat with a second layer of flour, egg, and crumbs. Chill for 2 hours or until ready to cook.

5 Heat the oil to 350°F and deep-fry the supremes in two batches for 10 minutes, carefully turning them over halfway. Drain and serve with new potatoes and a green vegetable such as broccoli or peas.

Mushroom and Parmesan Chicken

A VARIATION ON CHICKEN KIEV, IN THIS RECIPE THE CHICKEN IS STUFFED WITH MUSHROOMS AND PARSLEY RATHER THAN GARLIC BUTTER. USE OPEN MUSHROOMS WITH DARK GILLS SO THE FILLING CONTRASTS WELL WITH THE PALE FLESH OF THE CHICKEN AND COOK THEM UNTIL ANY EXCESS LIQUID HAS EVAPORATED.

SERVES 4

2 scallions
1 garlic clove
4 ounces mushrooms
1 tablespoon butter
3 tablespoons chopped fresh
    parsley
4 chicken breasts, skinned and
    boned
All-purpose flour, to dust
2 eggs, beaten
1 cup (3 ounces) fresh
    breadcrumbs
2 tablespoons finely shredded
    Parmesan cheese
Oil for deep-frying

1 Trim and thinly slice the scallions. Peel and crush the garlic and finely chop the mushrooms.

2 Heat the butter in a skillet and fry the onions for 1 minute. Stir in the garlic and mushrooms and cook for 2 minutes. Increase the heat under the pan slightly and continue to cook until the mushroom mixture is quite dry. Stir in 1 tablespoon of the chopped parsley and set aside to cool.

3 Cut a pocket in each chicken breast and fill with the mushroom mixture. Reshape the breasts so the filling is enclosed by the meat.

4 Coat the chicken in flour and brush with beaten egg. Mix together the breadcrumbs, Parmesan cheese, and remaining chopped parsley and press over the chicken until evenly covered. Chill for at least 30 minutes before cooking.

5 Heat oil for deep-frying to 350°F and fry the chicken for 10 minutes, turning the breasts over once. Drain and serve with mixed vegetables.

Turkey Croquettes with Pineapple and Red Currant Sauce

A FRUIT SAUCE, SUCH AS THIS ONE MADE WITH PINEAPPLE JUICE AND RED CURRANTS, PROVIDES A TANGY CONTRAST TO A MILDLY-FLAVORED MEAT LIKE TURKEY. IF PREFERRED, CRANBERRIES COULD BE USED INSTEAD OF RED CURRANTS OR SIMPLY SERVE THE CROQUETTES WITH TOMATO CHUTNEY OR KETCHUP.

SERVES 4

Croquettes:

6 scallions

3 ounces (6 tablespoons) butter

¾ cup (3½ ounces) all-purpose flour, plus extra to dust

1¼ cups (10 fluid ounces) milk

2 egg yolks

½ cup (2 ounces) shredded Cheddar cheese

12 ounces cooked turkey breast, ground

¾ cup (6 ounces) sweetcorn kernels

Salt and pepper

5 tablespoons dry breadcrumbs

1 tablespoon finely shredded Parmesan cheese

1 egg, beaten

Sauce:

5 tablespoons unsweetened pineapple juice

2 cups (9 ounces) fresh or frozen red currants or cranberries

½ cup (3 ounces) soft light brown sugar

Oil for deep-frying

1 Trim the scallions and chop finely. Heat the butter in a saucepan and fry the onions until softened. Remove the pan from the heat, blend in the flour, and stir in the milk.

2 Return the pan to a low heat and bring to a boil, stirring until smooth and thickened. Simmer for 1 minute, remove from the heat, and beat in the egg yolks and Cheddar cheese. Stir in the ground turkey and sweetcorn kernels, season with salt and pepper, and leave to cool.

3 Transfer the mixture to a bowl, cover and chill for 1 hour.

4 Mix together the dry breadcrumbs and Parmesan cheese. Divide the turkey mixture into 8 equal portions and shape into croquettes. Dust them with flour, brush with beaten egg, and coat in the crumbs and Parmesan. Chill again until ready to cook.

5 To make the sauce, simmer the pineapple juice, red currants, or cranberries, and sugar together in a pan for 10 minutes or until the fruit is soft, mashing occasionally with a fork.

6 Heat oil for deep-frying to 350°F and deep-fry the croquettes in two batches for 3 to 4 minutes until golden brown.

Herby Pork and Apple Patties

SERVE THESE TASTY PATTIES WITH MASHED POTATOES AND BROILED TOMATOES OR A MIXED SALAD.

SERVES 4

1 medium onion
1 apple, e.g., Baldwin, Cortland
1 pound ground pork
1 tablespoon chopped fresh
    sage
1 tablespoon Dijon mustard
Salt and pepper
All-purpose flour, for dusting
1 egg, beaten
⅔ cup (3 ounces) dry
    breadcrumbs
Oil for deep-frying

1 Peel and finely chop the onion. Peel, core, and finely chop or shred the apple.

2 In a bowl, mix together the pork meat, onion, apple, sage, and mustard. Season to taste.

3 With damp hands, shape the mixture into 12 small flat patties. Dust the patties with flour, brush with beaten egg, and press over the dry crumbs until each one is well coated. Place them on a plate in a single layer and chill for 1 hour.

4 Heat oil for deep-frying to 350°F and fry the patties for 6 to 7 minutes until cooked through. Drain and serve hot.

Pork with Orange and Tarragon Sauce

MATZO MEAL MAKES A CRISP, CRUNCHY COATING FOR MEAT AND FISH BUT DRY BREADCRUMBS COULD BE USED INSTEAD.

SERVES 4

¾ cup (4 ounces) matzo meal
1 teaspoon mixed dried herbs
All-purpose flour, to dust
8 thin pork steaks, total weight
    about 1½ pounds
1 egg, beaten
Oil for deep-frying

Sauce:
5 ounces button mushrooms
2 ounces (½ stick) butter
2 tablespoons cornstarch
1¼ cups (10 fluid ounces)
    chicken stock
Juice of ½ orange
1 teaspoon Dijon mustard
½ cup (4 fluid ounces) light cream
2 tablespoons chopped tarragon
Salt and pepper

1 Mix together the matzo meal and dried herbs. Dust the pork steaks with flour, brush with beaten egg, and press over the matzo meal to cover completely.

2 Heat oil for deep-frying to 350°F and fry the crumbed steaks in two batches for 4 to 5 minutes until golden brown and cooked through, turning over once. Drain and keep warm in a low oven while you make the sauce.

3 To make the sauce, quarter or slice the mushrooms. Melt the butter in a saucepan and fry the mushrooms for 2 to 3 minutes. Stir in the cornstarch off the heat, then blend in the chicken stock, orange juice, and mustard. Return to a low heat and stir until smooth and thickened. Simmer for 1 minute before stirring in the cream and tarragon.

4 Season the sauce with salt and pepper and spoon it over the pork. Serve with seasonal vegetables.

Turkey Cordon Bleu

THIS RECIPE CAN ALSO BE MADE WITH CHICKEN BREASTS, FOLLOWING THE METHOD GIVEN FOR THE CHICKEN KIEV RECIPE ON PAGE 68, BUT SUBSTITUTING THE HAM AND CHEESE SLICES FOR THE GARLIC BUTTER. SERVE WITH TOMATO AND MASCARPONE SAUCE OR ANOTHER TOMATO-BASED SAUCE.

SERVES 4

8 thin turkey steaks or turkey
    breast slices
4 thin slices of ham
4 thin slices of Gruyère cheese
⅔ cup (3 ounces) fresh
    breadcrumbs
1 tablespoon snipped fresh
    chives
All-purpose flour, to dust
1 egg, beaten
Oil for deep-frying

Sauce:
1¼ cups (10 fluid ounces)
    tomato pasta sauce
½ cup (4 ounces) mascarpone
    cheese
1 tablespoon snipped fresh chives

1 Lay the turkey between two sheets of plastic wrap and beat until thinner using a rolling pin or the flat side of a meat mallet.

2 Place four of the steaks on a board, top each one with a slice of ham and cheese and cover the filling by pressing the remaining steaks on top.

3 Mix together the breadcrumbs and chives and spread out on a plate. Dust the turkey with flour, brush with beaten egg, and coat with the crumb mix. Chill for 1 hour.

4 Heat about 1 inch oil to 335°F in a deep skillet and fry the turkey parcels, two at a time, for 8 to 10 minutes until golden brown, turning over half way.

5 While the turkey is cooking, gently warm the sauce ingredients without letting them boil, and stirring until the mascarpone is evenly blended in. Drain the turkey and serve with the sauce.

Cantonese Sweet and Sour Pork

A FAVORITE DISH IN CANTONESE RESTAURANTS AROUND THE WORLD. THE CHINESE WOULD USE
BELLY PORK BUT THIS RECIPE USES LEAN STEAKS CUT FROM THE SHOULDER OR LEG. A WOK CAN BE
USED TO COOK THE PORK AND THE VEGETABLES BUT, IF YOU PREFER, STIR-FRY THE VEGETABLES IN A
LARGE SKILLET.

SERVES 4

1 quantity (1 to 1½ cups) Beer
    Batter No 1 (see page 14)

Sweet and sour sauce:
½ cup (4 fluid ounces) chicken
    stock
3 tablespoons rice vinegar
1 tablespoon clear honey
3 tablespoons light soy sauce
2 tablespoons ketchup
1 teaspoon cornstarch

Pork:
1 pound pork steaks
Oil for deep-frying
All-purpose flour, to dust
1 garlic clove
1 yellow or orange bell pepper
8 scallions
8 lychees
4 tablespoons unsalted cashew
    nuts
1 teaspoon fresh ginger puree

1 Make up the batter and leave to stand for at least
   30 minutes.

2 To make the sauce, place all the ingredients except the
   cornstarch in a saucepan and heat gently. Mix the
   cornstarch with 1 tablespoon of water, add to the pan and
   stir continuously until the sauce is smooth and thickened.
   Simmer for 1 minute, then remove from the heat and
   set aside.

3 To cook the pork, cut the meat into 1-inch pieces. Heat
   oil in a wok or deep-fat fryer to 350°F. Dust the pork in
   flour, coat in the batter, and deep-fry for 3 to 4 minutes
   until golden brown and crisp. Drain and keep the pork
   warm in a low oven.

4 If using a wok, carefully pour off all but 2 tablespoons of
   the oil. If using a fryer, spoon off the same quantity of oil
   into a large skillet.

5 Peel and finely chop the garlic, seed and chop the pepper,
   trim and cut the scallions into 1-inch lengths. Peel the
   lychees and remove the pits.

6 Heat the oil in the wok or skillet and add the cashews. Stir-
   fry for 30 seconds until golden, then drain. Add the garlic,
   pepper, and ginger to the pan and stir-fry for 3 minutes.
   Add the scallions and lychees and stir-fry for 1 minute, and
   then add the pork.

7 Pour in the sauce, toss the ingredients together until coated
   and simmer for 2 minutes. Scatter over the cashews and
   serve immediately with fried or boiled rice and crispy
   seaweed (see page 102).

SPICE IT UP

There are endless ways to customize fried chicken. Try one of these options:

SMOKED PAPRIKA

In step 1, add ¼ cup **tomato paste**, 1 tablespoon **smoked paprika**, and 1 teaspoon **ground oregano** to buttermilk mixture.

SPICED MUSTARD

In step 1, add 1 tablespoon **ground mustard**, 4 teaspoons **Old Bay Seasoning**, and 2 to 3 teaspoons **hot sauce**, such as Tabasco, to buttermilk mixture.

LEMON-PEPPER GARLIC

In step 1, add 1 teaspoon **ground pepper**, 3 tablespoons **finely grated lemon zest** (from 3 lemons), and 4 **garlic cloves**, finely grated, to buttermilk mixture.

LIGHTEN UP
Love fried chicken?
Try our guilt-free
version (page 103).

classic fried chicken

SERVES 4 ■ ACTIVE TIME: 45 MIN ■ **TOTAL TIME: 45 MIN + MARINATING**

- ☐ 1¼ cups all-purpose flour
- ☐ ⅔ cup cornstarch
- ☐ coarse salt and ground pepper
- ☐ 1 quart buttermilk

- ☐ 1 chicken (3½ to 4 pounds), cut into 10 pieces, or 10 skin-on legs or thighs
- ☐ 3 cups vegetable oil

1 In a wide, shallow dish or pie plate, whisk together flour, cornstarch, 2 teaspoons salt, and ¼ teaspoon pepper. Transfer 1¼ cups flour mixture to an airtight container; set aside. In a large glass bowl, whisk together buttermilk, 2 tablespoons salt, and ¾ teaspoon pepper. Dredge chicken in flour mixture, then submerge in buttermilk mixture. Cover and refrigerate 3 hours (or up to overnight).

2 Place a wire rack on a rimmed baking sheet lined with paper towels. In a large cast-iron or other heavy skillet, heat oil to 350° over medium (a small cube of bread should brown in less than 1 minute). Transfer reserved flour mixture to a wide, shallow dish. In batches, lift chicken from buttermilk, letting excess drip off, and dredge in flour mixture.

3 Fry chicken until golden brown and cooked through, 16 to 20 minutes per batch, flipping once (adjust heat if browning too quickly). With tongs, transfer chicken to rack to drain, 5 minutes, then serve.

per serv: 750 cal; 33 g fat (8 g sat fat); 58 g protein; 52 g carb; 1 g fiber

Mixed Leaf Salad with Garlic Croutons and Shaved Parma Ham

A DELICIOUSLY CRUNCHY SALAD THAT HAS PLENTY OF STRONG FLAVORS. CHOOSE A CRUMBLY BLUE CHEESE SUCH AS ROQUEFORT OR STILTON AND A MIX OF DIFFERENT SALAD LEAVES— ROMAINE LETTUCE, ARUGULA, AND FRISEÉ ALL WORK WELL.

SERVES 4

2 large slices thick-cut sour dough or another country bread
4 slices Parma ham
2 garlic cloves
2 sticks celery
½ green bell pepper
8 ounces mixed salad leaves. e.g., Romaine lettuce, wild arugula, friseé, or iceberg lettuce
6 ounces blue cheese, e.g., Stilton, Roquefort
½ cup (2 ounces) walnut pieces
Oil for deep-frying

Dressing:
6 tablespoons extra virgin olive oil
2 tablespoons balsamic vinegar
Salt and pepper

1 Remove the crusts from the bread and cut into ½–inch croutons. Tear or cut the Parma ham into 1-inch strips. Peel the garlic, slice the celery, and chop the pepper.

2 Wash and dry the salad leaves and tear larger ones into bite-sized pieces. Cube or crumble the blue cheese and scatter over the leaves with the celery, pepper, and walnuts.

3 Heat 1 inch oil in a large skillet, add the garlic, and fry until the cloves turn golden brown. Fish them out with a slotted spoon and continue heating the oil until it reaches 350°F.

4 Fry the bread cubes for 2 minutes or until golden, then drain. Add the strips of Parma ham to the oil and fry for 1 to 2 minutes until crisp. Drain.

5 To make the dressing, whisk the olive oil, vinegar, and seasoning together and drizzle over the salad. Scatter over the croutons and crisp ham and serve.

Crispy Duck Rolls

SIMMERING THE DUCK BREASTS ENSURES THE MEAT STAYS TENDER AND SUCCULENT, WHEREAS IT CAN DRY OUT UNDER A BROILER. RESERVE THE COOKING LIQUID AND ONCE COLD, CHILL IT SO THE FAT SOLIDIFIES ON THE SURFACE. THIS CAN BE LIFTED OFF AND USED FOR FRYING POTATOES, WHILE THE STOCK CAN BE STORED IN THE FREEZER FOR ANOTHER RECIPE.

SERVES 4

3 small or 2 large duck breasts
2 bay leaves
8 black peppercorns
1 large onion
1 red bell pepper
4 ounces shiitake mushrooms
Oil for shallow and deep-frying
1 teaspoon shredded fresh
   ginger
4 ounces cucumber
3 tablespoons hoi sin sauce
1 tablespoon rice vinegar
12 spring roll wrappers
1 egg white, beaten

1 Place the duck breasts in a saucepan with the bay leaves and peppercorns and pour over cold water to cover. Bring to a boil, cover the pan, lower the heat, and simmer gently for 1 hour. Leave the duck to cool in the liquid, then drain, discard the skin, and chop the meat.

2 Peel and finely slice the onion, seed and chop the pepper, and chop or slice the mushrooms. Heat 2 tablespoons of oil in a skillet, add the onion, and cook gently until softened. Add the pepper, mushrooms, and ginger and fry for a further 5 minutes. Transfer to a bowl and leave to cool.

3 Cut the cucumber into small dice and add to the vegetables in the bowl with the duck, hoi sin sauce, and rice vinegar, stirring until mixed.

4 Place a spring roll wrapper on a board and top with a tablespoon of the duck mixture. Brush the edges of the wrapper with beaten egg white and roll up around the filling, tucking in the sides and pressing the edges together to seal. Repeat with the remaining wrappers and filling.

5 Heat oil to 350°F and deep-fry the rolls for 3 to 4 minutes until golden brown and crisp. Drain and serve hot with extra hoi sin sauce for dipping.

Lamb Pooris

GOLDEN CUSHIONS OF CRISP DOUGH BASED ON THE INDIAN BREAD CALLED POORI AND FILLED
WITH A RICH MIX OF LAMB AND VEGETABLES.

MAKES 20

Dough:

5 tablespoons (2½ ounces)
    butter
2 cups (8 ounces) all-purpose
    flour
Water to mix

Filling:

1 carrot
1 small parsnip
4 scallions
2 tablespoons oil, plus extra for
    deep-frying
8 ounces lean ground lamb
1 tablespoon curry paste
2 tablespoons tomato paste
1 cup (8 fluid ounces) lamb
    stock

1 To make the dough, cut up the butter into small pieces and
rub into the flour. Add ½ cup (4 fluid ounces) cold water to
mix to a soft dough. Knead the dough until smooth on a
lightly floured surface, then cover with plastic wrap and
chill for 30 minutes.

2 To make the filling, peel and cut the carrot and parsnip into
small pieces. Cook in a saucepan of boiling water for
5 minutes or until just tender. Drain.

3 Trim and chop the scallions. Heat 2 tablespoons of oil in a
skillet and fry the onions for 2 minutes until soft. Add the
ground lamb and fry until it browns, breaking up any
clumps of meat with a spoon.

4 Add the carrot and parsnip and stir in the curry paste and
tomato paste. Pour in the stock, bring to a boil, and simmer
for 15 minutes until the liquid has evaporated, stirring
occasionally so the meat doesn't stick to the pan. Allow
to cool.

5 Roll out the dough thinly on a floured surface. Using a
plain cutter, stamp out twenty 4-inch rounds, gathering
and re-rolling the dough trimmings as necessary. Dampen
the edges of the rounds with water and spoon a little of the
meat mixture on each. Fold the dough over the filling and
press the edges firmly together to seal.

6 Heat oil for deep-frying to 350°F and deep-fry the pooris
in batches for 3 to 4 minutes or until golden brown.
Drain and serve with mango chutney and a tomato and
cucumber salad.

Sesame Lamb in Potato Nests

IF YOU HAVE A WOK, USE IT TO DEEP-FRY THE POTATO NESTS AND THEN CAREFULLY POUR OFF THE EXCESS OIL BEFORE USING THE WOK TO STIR-FRY THE LAMB. IF NOT, FRY THE NESTS IN A LARGE SAUCEPAN OR DEEP-FAT FRYER AND USE A SKILLET TO COOK THE LAMB. THE NESTS CAN BE KEPT WARM ON A RACK IN A LOW OVEN WHILE THE LAMB COOKS.

SERVES 2

Potato nests:

2 medium (8 ounces) baking
    potatoes, e.g., Idaho
Oil for deep-frying

Sesame lamb:

½ red bell pepper
1 small zucchini
4 baby corn
12 ounces lean lamb
2 tablespoons hoi sin sauce
1 tablespoon dark soy sauce
2 tablespoons sesame oil
1 tablespoon sesame seeds

1 Peel the potatoes, coarsely shred or cut into wafer thin slices. Line a medium metal strainer (around 6 inches across) with half the potato strips and place another strainer or ladle on top to hold the potato in place.

2 Heat oil in a wok for deep-frying to 350°F, lower in the strainers and fry for 2 to 3 minutes or until the potato is golden brown. Remove the strainers from the oil and carefully lift out the potato basket. Drain and keep warm while you cook the second basket.

3 To cook the lamb, seed and slice the pepper, cut the zucchini into matchsticks, and halve the corn lengthways. Trim any fat from the lamb and cut into strips.

4 Carefully pour all but 2 tablespoons of the oil out of the wok and stir-fry the pepper, zucchini, and corn for 3 to 4 minutes. Remove from the pan and keep warm. Add the lamb to the wok and stir-fry over a brisk heat for 2 to 3 minutes. Pour in the hoi sin sauce and soy sauce, toss until the lamb is coated, and drizzle over the sesame oil.

5 Return the vegetables to the wok, stir-fry for 1 to 2 minutes, and then scatter over the sesame seeds. Transfer the potato baskets to serving plates and pile in the stir-fried lamb and vegetables. Serve at once.

Noodle Baskets with Black Bean Beef

THE BASKETS CAN BE MADE UP TO TWO DAYS IN ADVANCE, STORED IN AN AIRTIGHT CONTAINER IN THE REFRIGERATOR, AND THEN REHEATED IN A MODERATE OVEN WHEN NEEDED. REMEMBER TO USE METAL STRAINERS FOR FRYING THE BASKETS AS PLASTIC ONES WILL MELT IN THE HOT OIL.

SERVES 4

8 ounces thin egg noodles
Oil for deep-frying, plus
    2 tablespoons and extra
    for greasing

Black bean beef:
12 ounces sirloin or fillet steak,
    trimmed of fat
1 stick celery
½ yellow or orange bell pepper
4 cherry tomatoes
6 tablespoons Chinese black
    bean stir-fry sauce

1 Plunge the noodles into a saucepan of boiling water for 4 minutes until tender (or according to the packet instructions). Drain and rinse by running cold water through the strainer. Spread out the noodles on a tray and leave to dry.

2 Lightly oil a metal strainer, measuring roughly 5 inches in diameter, and line it with one quarter of the noodles. Press down in an even layer. Oil the base of a slightly smaller strainer and press down lightly on top of the noodles.

3 Heat oil for deep-frying to 375 °F in a wok or other wide, deep pan. Hold the handles of the strainers together (protect your hand with an oven mitt) and lower the strainers into the oil. Cook for about 3 minutes or until the noodles are crisp and golden.

4 Remove the strainers from the oil and carefully lift out the top one. Run a knife around the noodle basket to loosen it, turn the strainer over and tap carefully to release the basket. Make three more baskets in the same way.

5 For the beef, cut the steak into thin strips, slice the celery and pepper, and halve the tomatoes. Heat 2 tablespoons of oil in a wok or large skillet and stir-fry the steak over a high heat for 2 to 3 minutes.

6 Remove the beef from the pan, add the celery and pepper, and stir-fry for 3 minutes. Add the cherry tomato halves and stir-fry for 1 minute. Return the beef to the pan, pour in the black bean sauce, and toss the meat and vegetables together until coated with the sauce and piping hot. Spoon into the baskets and serve.

4 | fish & shellfish

As fish and shellfish have such delicate flesh, it is especially important to give them a protective coating before deep-frying. The coating not only prevents the fish over-cooking and drying out during frying but also helps to trap any juices inside the flesh, keeping it moist and stopping the juices from leaking out and tainting the oil. Breadcrumbs, batter, polenta, or oatmeal all make good coatings for fish and shellfish and these can be flavored with herbs, spices, citrus rind, or sesame seeds.

Lemon and Herb Sardines   ILLUSTRATED RIGHT

ASK YOUR FISH MERCHANT TO SCALE, CLEAN, AND REMOVE THE SARDINE HEADS. SPLIT THE FISH
OPEN ALONG THE UNDERSIDE, LAY THEM SKIN SIDE UP ON A BOARD, AND PRESS YOUR THUMBS
DOWN THE BACK TO LOOSEN THE BONES, SNIPPING THE BACKBONE JUST ABOVE THE TAIL WITH
SCISSORS. TURN THEM OVER AND GENTLY PULL AWAY THE BACK AND RIB BONES IN ONE STEP.

SERVES 4

12 sardines, split open and
    filleted
All-purpose flour, to dust
1 egg
2 tablespoons milk
2 cups (6 ounces) fresh
    breadcrumbs
1 tablespoon finely chopped
    fresh parsley
1 tablespoon finely chopped
    tarragon
Oil for deep-frying

To serve:
Lemon wedges

1 Dust the sardines with flour. Beat the egg and milk together
  in a shallow dish. Mix the breadcrumbs with the parsley and
  tarragon and spread out on a plate.

2 Dip the sardines in the egg and milk mixture and coat well
  with the crumbs.

3 Heat oil for deep-frying to 350°F and fry the sardines in
  batches for 2 to 3 minutes or until golden. Drain and serve
  at once with wedges of lemon to squeeze over.

Herrings in Oatmeal

OATMEAL MAKES A LIGHT CRISP COATING IN THIS TRADITIONAL SCOTTISH DISH. THE COATING CAN
ALSO BE USED FOR OTHER FIRM FISH FILLETS SUCH AS SOLE, MACKEREL, OR COD.

SERVES 2

2 herrings, filleted
3 tablespoons all-purpose flour
¼ teaspoon mustard powder
Pinch of salt
6 tablespoons medium oatmeal
1 teaspoon dried thyme
1 egg, beaten
Oil for deep-frying
Lemon wedges, to serve

1 Rinse the herring fillets and pat dry with a paper towel. Mix
  together the flour, mustard, and salt. On a separate plate,
  mix together the oatmeal and thyme.

2 Coat the herrings in the flour mix, dip in the beaten egg,
  and coat with the oatmeal, pressing it firmly over the fish.
  Chill for 30 minutes or until ready to cook.

3 Heat oil for deep-frying to 350°F and fry the herring fillets,
  two at a time, for 3 to 4 minutes until golden brown,
  turning over half way.

4 Drain and garnish with lemon wedges to squeeze over. Serve
  with new potatoes and peas.

Traditional English Fried Fish ILLUSTRATED LEFT

YEAST BATTER WORKS PARTICULARLY WELL WITH FRIED FISH, AS IT STAYS CRISP TO THE LAST BITE!

SERVES 4

1½ pounds firm white fish
    fillets, e.g., cod or haddock
Salt and pepper
All-purpose flour, for coating
1 quantity (about 1 cup) of yeast
    batter (see page 14)
Oil for deep-frying

To garnish:
Fried parsley (see page 111)
Lemon wedges
English-style "chip shop"
    French fries (see page 119)

1 Skin the fish fillets and cut into four equal portions. Season with salt and pepper.

2 Dust the fillets with flour and then dip in the batter until well coated.

3 Heat oil for deep-frying to 375°F. Fry the fish in the hot oil, two fillets at a time, for about 5 minutes or until golden brown. Drain and keep warm.

4 Garnish the fish with the deep-fried parsley sprigs and lemon wedges, and serve with French fries.

Pecan-crusted Sole Goujons

FRESH BREADCRUMBS CAN BE MADE WHENEVER YOU HAVE LEFT-OVER BREAD. REDUCE THE BREAD TO CRUMBS IN A FOOD PROCESSOR (WITH OR WITHOUT CRUSTS), AND FREEZE IN TIGHTLY SEALED BAGS. MARK THE WEIGHT OF CRUMBS ON THE OUTSIDE OF THE BAG UNTIL NEEDED.

SERVES 4

1 cup (3 ounces) fresh
    breadcrumbs
2 tablespoons finely chopped
    pecans
2 tablespoons finely shredded
    hard cheese, e.g., Cheddar
    or Monteray Jack
Salt and pepper
1¼ pounds sole fillets, cut into
    3–inch strips
All-purpose flour, for dusting
4 tablespoons mayonnaise
2 tablespoons chopped fresh
    tarragon
Oil for deep-frying
Lemon wedges, to serve

1 Mix together the breadcrumbs, chopped pecans, and shredded cheese and spread out on a large plate. Season the strips of fish and dust lightly with flour.

2 In a shallow dish, mix together the mayonnaise and tarragon. Add the fish and stir until coated.

3 Lift out the pieces of sole and toss in the crumbs. Spread out on a plate and chill for 30 minutes.

4 Deep-fry the sole in hot oil at 350°F for 2 to 3 minutes until golden brown. Drain and serve hot, garnished with lemon wedges.

Devilled Smelt with Gremolata ILLUSTRATED RIGHT

GREMOLATA IS A TANGY MIX OF PARSLEY, GARLIC, AND LEMON RIND THAT THE ITALIANS SPRINKLE OVER FULL FLAVORED MEAT DISHES LIKE OSSOBUCO. IT ALSO WORKS WELL WITH FISH.

SERVES 4

Gremolata:
Rind of 1 lemon, finely shredded
3 tablespoons finely chopped flat-leaf parsley
2 garlic cloves, finely chopped

Smelt:
½ cup (4 ounces) all-purpose flour
½ teaspoon hot chili powder
Salt and pepper
1½ pounds smelt
Oil for deep-frying

1 For the gremolata, mix the lemon rind, parsley, and garlic together in a small dish.

2 For the fish, put the flour, chili powder, and salt and pepper to taste in a large plastic food bag. Rinse the smelt in a colander, pat dry, and add to the bag. Shake quite vigorously so the fish is coated with the flour.

3 Heat oil for deep-frying to 375°F. Deep-fry the fish in three or four batches for about 3 minutes each until the fish are crisp and pale golden.

4 Drain and serve sprinkled with the gremolata.

Fritto Misto

FRIED FISH ITALIAN STYLE; THIS IS A PARTICULARLY POPULAR DISH ALONG THE COAST OF NAPLES WHERE LOCAL CATCHES ENSURE AN ABUNDANCE OF SEAFOOD.

SERVES 4

2 cups (8 ounces) self-rising flour, plus extra for dusting
½ teaspoon baking soda
Salt and pepper
1¼ cups (10 fluid ounces) water
2 pounds mixed seafood, e.g., large shrimp, baby squid, white fish fillets
Oil for deep-frying

To serve:
2 anchovy fillets, chopped
1 tablespoon chopped capers
1 tablespoon chopped baby gherkins
8 tablespoons mayonnaise

1 Sift the self-rising flour and baking soda into a bowl and season with salt and pepper. Make a well in the center, pour in half the water and stir until mixed. Gradually stir in the rest of the water to make a smooth batter.

2 Prepare the seafood by peeling the shrimp (leave the tails on) and cutting the fish fillets into small pieces.

3 Heat oil for deep-frying to 350°F. Dust the prepared seafood in flour, dip in the batter and fry in the hot oil for 2 to 3 minutes until golden brown.

4 To serve, chop the anchovies, capers, and gherkins and stir into the mayonnaise. Drain the seafood and serve at once with the mayonnaise.

Salt and Pepper Squid

BEFORE FRYING THE SQUID, SCORE THE FLESH WITH A SHARP KNIFE IN A LATTICE PATTERN SO THE PIECES CURL ATTRACTIVELY AS THEY COOK. TAKE CARE NOT TO CUT TOO DEEPLY, HOWEVER, AS THE FLESH IS DELICATE AND YOU COULD END UP SHREDDING IT!

SERVES 4

Dressing:
½ teaspoon sweet chili sauce
½ teaspoon crushed garlic
1 teaspoon brown sugar
Juice of 2 limes
6 tablespoons Thai fish sauce

Squid:
2 teaspoons freshly ground
    white pepper
1 teaspoon salt
1 cup (4 ounces) all-purpose
    flour
2 garlic cloves
Oil for deep-frying
1 pound 2 ounces (cleaned
    weight) medium sized squid,
    scored
2 tablespoons chopped fresh
    cilantro

1 For the dressing, whisk together the chili sauce, garlic, brown sugar, lime juice, and fish sauce.

2 For the squid, mix the pepper, salt, and flour together in a bowl. Peel the garlic cloves and leave whole.

3 Heat oil for deep-frying to 350°F. Toss the squid in the seasoned flour until it is well coated and add about a quarter to the hot oil. Fry for 4 to 5 minutes until the squid curls and becomes crisp. Drain and keep warm in a low oven while you fry the remainder in three batches.

4 Divide the squid between serving plates and scatter over the cilantro. Drizzle the dressing around the squid.

5 Serve at once with a little salt sprinkled over, garnished with lemon wedges.

Gingered Crab Cakes

VARY THE AMOUNT OF CHILE PEPPER ACCORDING TO PERSONAL TASTE—ADD MORE IF YOU WANT THE CRAB CAKES TO HAVE A REAL KICK, LESS IF YOU DON'T WANT THEM TOO HOT.

SERVES 4

5 medium (1¼ pounds) baking
  potatoes, e.g., Idaho
Salt and pepper
4 scallions
1 red or green chile pepper
8 anchovy fillets
1½ teaspoons crushed garlic
1 teaspoon shredded fresh
  ginger
Rind of 1 lime, finely shredded
2 tablespoons chopped fresh
  cilantro
2 tablespoons snipped fresh
  chives
14 ounces white crab meat
All-purpose flour, for dusting
2 eggs, beaten
1 cup (3 ounces) fresh
  breadcrumbs
Oil for deep-frying

1 Peel the potatoes, cut into even-size pieces, and cook in a saucepan of boiling, salted water until tender. Drain, mash, and leave to cool.

2 Chop the scallions, seed and finely chop the chile pepper, and snip the anchovies into small pieces with scissors. Stir the onions, chile pepper, and anchovies into the potatoes with the garlic, ginger, lime rind, cilantro, chives, and crab meat. Season to taste with salt and pepper.

3 Shape the mixture into 12 balls, place on a plate and chill for 30 minutes. Dust the crab cakes with flour, brush with beaten egg and coat in the breadcrumbs.

4 Deep fry in hot oil at 335°F for 7 to 8 minutes until golden brown. Drain and serve at once with tartare sauce or lemon mayonnaise.

Tempura Shrimp in Barbecue Sauce

SMALL CHUNKS OF FIRM WHITE FISH CAN ALSO BE COOKED USING THE SAME METHOD
DEMONSTRATED BELOW. IF USING FROZEN SHRIMP, DEFROST THEM THOROUGHLY AND
PAT DRY WITH PAPER TOWELS BEFORE DIPPING THEM IN THE BATTER AND DEEP-FRYING.

SERVES 4

16 large raw shrimp
1 red bell pepper
1 green bell pepper
Oil for deep-frying
1 quantity (about 2 cups)
    Tempura Batter (see
    page 14)

Barbecue sauce:
1 tablespoon sweet chili sauce
2 tablespoons light soy sauce
1 tablespoon sugar
2 tablespoons rice vinegar
4 tablespoons ketchup
1 cup (8 fluid ounces) chicken
    stock
1 tablespoon cornstarch

1 Shell the shrimp, removing the heads but leaving the tails on if preferred. Cut down the back of each shrimp and pull out the black thread running down it. Rinse the shrimp and pat dry with a paper towel.

2 Seed and slice the peppers.

3 Heat oil for deep-frying to 350°F. Dip the shrimp and pepper slices in the batter and deep-fry in batches in the hot oil for 3 to 4 minutes or until golden and crisp.

4 To make the barbecue sauce, mix the chili sauce, light soy sauce, sugar, rice vinegar, ketchup, and chicken stock together in a saucepan. Blend the cornstarch with 3 tablespoons water until smooth, add to the pan, and bring to a boil over a low heat, stirring constantly. Simmer for 1 minute.

5 Drain the shrimp and peppers and serve with the sauce spooned over the egg noodles.

Spiced Squid Rings with Jalapeno Salsa

MARINATE THE SQUID RINGS FOR SEVERAL HOURS BEFORE COOKING TO HELP TENDERIZE THEM AND ADD EXTRA FLAVOR.

SERVES 4

1 pound cleaned squid, cut into
    rings
2 large garlic cloves
3 tablespoons olive oil
3 tablespoons lemon juice
1 teaspoon paprika
All-purpose flour, to dust
2 teaspoons curry paste
1 quantity (about 1 cup) Yeast
    Batter or Beer Batter No 2
    (see page 14)
Oil for deep-frying

Salsa:
1 red onion
2 medium tomatoes
1 fresh or bottled green
    jalapeno pepper
2 garlic cloves
1 tablespoon chopped fresh
    parsley
Salt and pepper
4 tablespoons olive oil
1 tablespoon white wine vinegar

1 Put the squid in a bowl. Peel and crush the garlic and mix with the olive oil, lemon juice, and paprika. Pour over the squid, stir until the rings are coated, and leave to marinate for 3 to 4 hours.

2 Drain the squid and dust with flour. Stir the curry paste into the batter.

3 Heat oil for deep-frying to 350°F. Coat the squid rings in the batter and deep-fry for about 2 minutes or until golden and crisp. Drain.

4 To make the salsa, peel and finely chop the onion. Chop the tomatoes, seed and finely chop the jalapeno pepper, peel and finely chop the garlic. Mix the onion, tomatoes, pepper, garlic, and parsley together and season with salt and pepper. Whisk the olive oil and vinegar together and pour over.

5 Pile the squid rings on serving plates and serve with the salsa.

Mussel Fritters with Tartare Sauce ILLUSTRATED RIGHT

SERVE THESE AS A LIGHT MEAL WITH THE SAUCE IN A SMALL DISH ALONGSIDE. GARNISH EACH PLATE WITH QUARTERED CHERRY TOMATOES, CHOPPED RADISHES, AND CUCUMBER.

SERVES 4

20 large mussels, e.g., Green Lip
All-purpose flour, to dust
Oil for deep-frying
1 quantity (about 1½ cups) Beer
　　Batter No 1 (see page 14)

Tartare sauce:
6 tablespoons mayonnaise
1 tablespoon finely chopped
　　gherkins
2 teaspoons chopped capers
1 tablespoon chopped fresh
　　parsley

1 Rinse the mussels and pat dry with paper towels. Dust lightly with flour.

2 Heat oil for deep-frying to 350°F. Dip the mussels in the batter and fry in the oil for 2 to 3 minutes or until golden brown and crisp.

3 To make the sauce, mix together the mayonnaise, gherkins, capers, and parsley and spoon into individual dishes.

4 Drain the mussels and serve hot with the Tartare Sauce and cherry tomato salad.

Cod with Gingered Hoi Sin Sauce

HOI SIN IS A CHINESE SAUCE USED FOR GLAZING SPARE RIBS AND CHICKEN WINGS AND IT MAKES AN EXCELLENT DIP FOR SPRING ROLLS.

SERVES 4

1¼ pound cod fillet
All-purpose flour, to dust
1 red onion
1 red bell pepper
2 garlic cloves
2 ounces snow peas
Oil for stir-frying and deep-
　　frying
1 quantity (about 1½ to 2 cups)
　　Simple Flour and Water
　　Batter (see page 14)
1 teaspoon fresh ginger puree
6 tablespoons hoi sin sauce
2 tablespoons rice vinegar
2 tablespoons light soy sauce

1 Cut the fish into 1½-inch pieces and dust with flour.

2 Peel and slice the onion, seed and chop the pepper, peel and finely chop the garlic, and slice the snow peas lengthways into three or four strips.

3 Heat 2 tablespoons of oil in a skillet, add the onion, pepper, and ginger and stir-fry for 3 minutes. Add the snow peas and garlic and stir-fry for 2 minutes. Stir in the hoi sin sauce, rice vinegar, and soy sauce and leave to simmer over a gentle heat while you cook the fish.

4 Heat oil for deep-frying to 350°F. Stir the batter and add half the fish pieces to it. Lift them out one by one, add to the hot oil and fry for 3 to 4 minutes until they are crisp. Drain and fry the remaining fish in the same way.

5 Serve the sauce and vegetables spooned over the fish with boiled or fried rice.

Tuna, Shrimp, and Potato Cakes with Avocado Salsa

TUNA WORKS WELL IN THIS RECIPE AS IT HAS A FIRM, DENSE TEXTURE BUT OTHER FISH SUCH AS HADDOCK, SOLE, OR SALMON COULD ALSO BE USED.

SERVES 4

9 ounces fresh tuna fillet
3-4 medium (14 ounces) baking
 potatoes, e.g., Idaho
2 ounces (½ stick) butter
1 tablespoon chopped fresh dill
2 egg yolks
Salt and pepper
16 cooked shrimp, peeled
All-purpose flour, to dust
2 eggs, beaten
1 cup (3 ounces) fresh
 breadcrumbs
Oil for deep-frying

Salsa:
1 avocado
2 tomatoes
Juice of 1 lime
1 tablespoon olive oil
Dash of Tabasco

1 Broil or pan-fry the tuna for about 5 minutes or until just cooked through. Leave to cool, then remove any skin and finely flake or chop the flesh.

2 Peel the potatoes, cut into chunks, and cook in a saucepan of boiling water until tender. Drain and mash with the butter. Add the dill and egg yolks, season with salt and pepper, and stir in the tuna.

3 Leave to cool and then shape the mixture into 16 oval cakes. Press a shrimp into the center of each, covering the shrimp completely. Dust the cakes with flour, brush with beaten egg, and coat in the breadcrumbs. Chill for 30 minutes.

4 Heat oil for deep-frying to 350°F and fry the cakes in batches for 5 minutes or until crisp and golden. Drain.

5 To make the salsa, halve the avocado, remove the pit, peel and chop the flesh. Skin, seed, and chop the tomatoes and mix with the avocado, lime juice, olive oil, and Tabasco. Serve the salsa with the hot tuna and potato cakes.

5 | vegetables

Deep-fried vegetables are a popular part of most cuisines, turning up as pakoras in India, fried seaweed in China, sweetcorn cakes in Thailand, or tempura in Japan. The vegetables are usually cut into small pieces before being coated in batter, crumbs, or choux paste, so only need frying for a short time to become deliciously light and crisp on the outside but still retain a little "bite" in the middle.

Crisp and Crunchy Onion Rings

LARGE SWEET ONIONS WORK BEST FOR THIS RECIPE. THE RINGS CAN BE SERVED ON THEIR OWN, WITH A MUSTARD, SPICY TOMATO, OR SOUR CREAM DIP, OR AS A GARNISH FOR BURGERS, STEAKS, AND MEATLOAF.

SERVES 4

1 large white onion
All-purpose flour, to dust
1 egg white
1 cup (5 ounces) matzo meal or
   fine cornmeal
½ teaspoon ground cumin
Oil for deep-frying

1 Peel the onion and cut into ¼-inch slices. Separate each slice into individual rings.

2 Dust the rings with flour. Lightly beat the egg white. Mix the matzo meal or cornmeal with the cumin and spread out on a plate.

3 Dip the onion rings in the egg white and then coat in the matzo meal.

4 Heat oil for deep-frying to 350°F and fry the onion rings in batches for 1 to 2 minutes or until crisp and golden. Drain and serve hot.

Autumn Vegetable Beignets

SERVE THESE AS A STARTER OR LIGHT MEAL AND VARY THE MIXTURE OF VEGETABLES ACCORDING TO WHAT YOU HAVE AVAILABLE.

SERVES 4

1½ pounds mixed autumn
   vegetables, e.g., rutabaga,
   carrot, parsnip, squash
Oil for roasting and deep-frying
9 ounces cooked beetroot
1 teaspoon mixed dried herbs
1 quantity (about 2 to 2½ cups)
   Beer Batter No 2 (see page
   14)

1 Prepare the mixed vegetables by peeling and seeding as necessary. Cut into two-bite size pieces.

2 Preheat the oven to 400°F. Spread out the vegetables in a shallow roasting pan, drizzle with 2 or 3 tablespoons of oil, and turn until coated. Roast for 30 minutes or until the vegetables are tender. Leave to cool.

3 Peel the beetroot and cut into wedges.

4 Heat oil for deep-frying to 375°F. Stir the dried herbs into the batter and add the roasted vegetables, mixing until coated. Deep-fry in batches for 1 to 2 minutes until golden. Drain and keep warm. Once they have all been fried, dip the beetroot in the batter and fry for 1 to 2 minutes.

5 Serve at once with mustard mayonnaise.

ILLUSTRATED: Crisp and Crunchy Onion Rings

Chinese Crispy "Seaweed"

IN CHINA, COOKS WOULD MAKE THIS DISH WITH SEAWEED BUT UNFORTUNATELY THE TYPE THEY
USE IS NOT YET AVAILABLE IN THE WEST. HOWEVER, YOUNG CABBAGE, BOK CHOY, OR SPINACH
LEAVES CAN ALL BE SUBSTITUTED AND WORK EQUALLY WELL. STAND WELL BACK WHEN YOU ADD
THE SHREDDED LEAVES TO THE HOT OIL AS MOISTURE IN THE LEAVES WILL CAUSE IT TO SPIT.
SERVE THE "SEAWEED" AS PART OF A CHINESE MEAL.

SERVES 4

2 garlic cloves
9 ounces green cabbage or
    spinach leaves
Oil for deep-frying
1 teaspoon salt
1 teaspoon sugar

1 Skin the garlic and cut the cloves into wafer thin slices.
Remove any tough stalks from the cabbage or spinach leaves
and rinse well in cold water. Drain and dry thoroughly with
paper towels.

2 Roll up the leaves tightly, one or two at a time, and slice very
thinly with a sharp knife, about ⅛–inch thick.

3 Heat oil for deep-frying to 350°F and deep-fry the shredded
greens, a handful at a time, for about 30 seconds until they
turn dark green and crisp. Drain each batch before you fry
the next.

4 Add the garlic with the last batch of greens, drain and toss
with the rest of the fried leaves. Sprinkle with the salt and
sugar and serve.

Split Pea Fritters with Roasted Red Bell Pepper Sauce

SERVE THIS FOR AN APPETIZER OR AS PART OF A VEGETARIAN MEAL. THE SPLIT PEAS NEED TO BE SOAKED OVERNIGHT SO THEY CAN BE GROUND TO A MEAL IN A FOOD PROCESSOR.

SERVES 4

Red bell pepper sauce:

2 large red bell peppers

1 tablespoon sun-dried tomato paste

About 1½ cups (12 fluid ounces) vegetable stock

Fritters:

1½ cups (8 ounces) yellow split peas

1 small red onion

1 large garlic clove

1 tablespoon whole wheat flour

2 tablespoons chopped fresh cilantro

½ teaspoon ground turmeric

½ teaspoon ground cumin

1 teaspoon baking powder

Salt and pepper

Oil for deep-frying

To garnish:

Deep-fried basil leaves

1 For the sauce, line a broiler pan with aluminum foil. Place the peppers on it and broil them on all sides until their skins are scorched and black. Wrap the foil around the peppers and fold over the edges to make a tightly sealed parcel. Leave until cool enough to handle, then unwrap the peppers, remove the stalks and seeds, and strip off the skins.

2 Place the skinned peppers in a food processor or blender with the tomato paste and half the stock. Blend to a paste, adding enough of the remaining stock to make a smooth sauce (the amount of stock needed will depend on the size of your peppers). Keep the sauce in a covered bowl in the refrigerator until needed.

3 Place the split peas in a bowl, cover with cold water, and leave to soak overnight. Drain and grind the peas to a fine meal in a food processor. Peel and very finely chop the onion and crush the garlic.

4 Transfer the split pea meal to a bowl and stir in the onion, garlic, whole wheat flour, cilantro, turmeric, cumin, baking powder, and seasoning. Beat the mixture with a wooden spoon until light and fluffy.

5 With damp hands, roll the mixture into small balls. Heat oil for deep-frying to 350°F and fry in several batches for 4 to 5 minutes until golden brown.

6 Drain, warm the red bell pepper sauce, and serve with the hot fritters.

Falafel

THESE CAN BE SERVED AS NIBBLES AT A PARTY OR AS A VEGETARIAN SNACK PILED INTO PITA BREAD WITH SALAD. IF SERVING AS NIBBLES, ACCOMPANY WITH HUMMUS OR A YOGURT AND MINT DIP.

SERVES 4

1 red onion
2 large garlic cloves
Salt and pepper
Two 14–ounce cans of
    chickpeas, drained
1 tablespoon ground coriander
2 teaspoons ground cumin
1 teaspoon paprika
2 tablespoons chopped fresh
    parsley
1 egg, beaten
All-purpose flour, for dusting
Oil for deep-frying

1 Peel the onion and chop finely. Peel the garlic and crush with a little salt.

2 Grind the chickpeas to a meal in a food processor or mash in a bowl. Stir in the onion, garlic, coriander, cumin, paprika, and parsley and season with pepper. Mix in the beaten egg until evenly combined.

3 Roll the mixture into small oval-shaped balls, dust with flour and flatten slightly. Chill for 1 hour.

4 Heat oil for deep-frying to 350°F and fry the falafel, four at a time, for 3 to 4 minutes until golden. Drain and serve warm.

Quesadillas

THESE CHEESE-FILLED TURNOVERS ARE A POPULAR SNACK IN MEXICO. USE A MIX OF TWO CONTRASTING CHEESES.

MAKES 8

½ red bell pepper
½ green bell pepper
1¾ cups (7 ounces) shredded
    mature Cheddar cheese
1¾ cups (7 ounces) crumbled
    feta cheese
1 teaspoon smoked paprika
2 tablespoons chopped fresh
    cilantro
8 whole wheat tortillas, about 6
    inches in diameter
1 egg, beaten
Oil for deep-frying

1 Broil the pepper skins until they scorch and blacken, wrap in aluminum foil until cool enough to handle, then strip away the skins. Chop the peppers into small dice.

2 In a bowl, mix together the peppers, Cheddar, feta, paprika, and cilantro. Divide the mixture between the tortillas, brush the edges with beaten egg, and fold in half to enclose the filling, pressing the edges together to seal.

3 Heat about 1 inch of oil in a large deep skillet to 350°F and fry the quesadillas for 2 to 3 minutes on each side until crisp and golden brown. Drain and serve hot with a green salad.

Indian Pakoras with Cilantro Raita

INDIAN COOKS WOULD MAKE THESE FRITTERS WITH BESAN (CHICKPEA FLOUR) BUT IF YOU HAVE PROBLEMS TRACKING IT DOWN, PLAIN WHOLE WHEAT FLOUR COULD BE SUBSTITUTED. USE A MIX OF DIFFERENT VEGETABLES AND PREPARE THEM AS NECESSARY. FIRMER ONES SUCH AS CAULIFLOWER FLORETS, BAKING POTATOES, AND CARROTS NEED TO BE BLANCHED UNTIL THEY ARE JUST TENDER, WHILE SOFTER ONES SUCH AS EGGPLANT AND ZUCCHINI CAN SIMPLY BE CUT INTO CHUNKS. GARAM MASALA IS A SPICE MIX AVAILABLE FROM LARGER SUPERMARKETS AND INDIAN STORES.

SERVES 4

1¾ cups (8 ounces) besan
    (chickpea flour) or plain
    whole wheat flour
½ teaspoon salt
1 teaspoon garam masala
1 teaspoon ground coriander
1 teaspoon cumin seeds
½ teaspoon chili powder
2 cups (16 fluid ounces) cold
    water
2 egg whites
2 pounds mixed vegetables,
    e.g., cauliflower florets,
    eggplant, baking potatoes,
    baby carrots, broccoli
    florets, zucchini
Oil for deep-frying
All-purpose flour, for dusting

Raita:
6 tablespoons thick plain yogurt
2 tablespoons chopped fresh
    cilantro
½ teaspoon black mustard seeds

1 Mix the flour, salt, garam masala, coriander, cumin seeds, and chili powder in a bowl. Add enough water to mix to a smooth batter that has the consistency of unwhipped heavy cream.

2 Leave the batter to stand for 1 hour or until ready to cook.

3 Whisk the egg whites until standing in soft peaks and fold into the batter. Cut the vegetables into bite-size pieces.

4 Heat oil for deep-frying to 375°F. Dust the vegetables with flour and coat in batter, one piece at a time so they don't clump together, and fry in the hot oil for about 3 minutes until crisp and golden brown.

5 To make the raita, mix the yogurt and cilantro together and sprinkle with the mustard seeds. Drain the vegetables and serve hot with the raita.

Crispy Noodles with Chinese Vegetables

THIS RECIPE IS A GOOD WAY OF USING UP ANY LEFTOVER COOKED NOODLES. DRIED EGG NOODLES COULD ALSO BE USED BUT THEY WILL NEED TO BE COOKED FIRST.

SERVES 4

Oil for deep-frying
8 ounces cooked egg noodles
1½ pounds mixed vegetables,
    e.g., bell peppers, snow
    peas, baby corn, zucchinis,
    mushrooms
1 tablespoon sunflower oil
1 tablespoon sesame oil
1 tablespoon lemon juice
2 tablespoons light soy sauce
2 tablespoons oyster sauce

1 Heat oil for deep-frying to 375°F—make sure you heat the oil to the correct temperature or the cooked noodles will be tough and chewy rather than crisp.

2 Cut the noodles into short lengths and deep-fry in batches for 2 to 3 minutes until golden and crisp. Drain and keep warm in the oven.

3 Prepare the vegetables as necessary and cut into bite-size pieces. Heat the sunflower and sesame oils in a wok or large skillet and stir-fry the vegetables for 6 to 8 minutes until they start to soften.

4 Mix together the lemon juice, soy sauce, and oyster sauce and pour over the vegetables. Stir-fry for another minute, tossing the vegetables so they are coated with the sauce. Serve piled on top of the crisp noodles.

Melanzane in Carrozza

EGGPLANT SLICES LAYERED WITH MOZZARELLA, DIPPED IN BATTER, AND DEEP-FRIED UNTIL CRISP MAKE AN UNUSUAL LIGHT LUNCH. ACCOMPANY WITH A TANGY TOMATO AND BASIL SALAD.

SERVES 2

1 large eggplant
Freshly ground black pepper
Olive oil for brushing
6 slices mozzarella cheese
All-purpose flour, to dust
1 teaspoon Italian-style dried
    mixed herbs
1 quantity (about 1½ to 2 cups)
    Beer Batter No 2 (See
    page 14)
Oil for deep-frying

1 Cut the eggplant into 12 thin slices, season them with pepper, and brush with olive oil. Sear in a heavy ridged broiler pan until just tender.

2 Leave the eggplant slices to cool. Sandwich the mozzarella cheese between the eggplant slices and dust with flour. Stir the herbs into the batter.

3 Heat oil for deep-frying to 350°F, dip the mozzarella sandwiches in the batter until evenly coated, and fry for 2 minutes, turning over after 1 minute, until golden and crisp on both sides. Drain and serve hot with a tomato and basil salad.

Eggplant Fritters with Eggplant Paté

EGGPLANT PATÉS ARE POPULAR IN THE MIDDLE EAST WHERE THE EGGPLANTS ARE COOKED OVER AN OPEN FLAME TO GIVE THEM A SMOKY, CHARGRILLED FLAVOR. IN THIS RECIPE THEY ARE BAKED IN A CONVENTIONAL OVEN BUT THEY COULD ALSO BE COOKED ON A BARBECUE.

SERVES 4

Paté:
2 medium eggplants
1 slice of bread
2 garlic cloves
1 tablespoon lemon juice
1 tablespoon chopped fresh
    parsley
4 tablespoons extra virgin
    olive oil
Salt and pepper

Fritters:
1 large eggplant
2 tablespoons all-purpose flour
1 quantity (about 1½ cups) Beer
    Batter No 1 (see page 14)
Oil for deep-frying

1 For the paté, preheat the oven to 400°F. Score the eggplants round the center with a sharp knife and place them on a lightly greased baking sheet. Cook in the oven for about 40 minutes or until tender.

2 Cut the eggplants in half and scoop out the flesh with a spoon. Soak the bread in a little water for 5 minutes. Skin and roughly chop the garlic. Squeeze out the bread and place in a food processor with the eggplant flesh, garlic, lemon juice, parsley, and olive oil.

3 Blend together until smooth and creamy and season with salt and pepper to taste.

4 For the fritters, top and tail the eggplant and cut into ¼-inch slices. Dust with the flour. Heat oil for deep-frying to 350°F.

5 Dip the eggplant slices in the batter and deep fry in batches, 3 or 4 at a time, for 1 to 2 minutes on each side or until golden brown and crisp. Drain and keep warm in a low oven until all the slices have been cooked.

6 Serve with the eggplant paté (gently reheated in a small pan or in the microwave, if necessary) and roasted vine tomatoes.

Veggie Beanburgers ILLUSTRATED RIGHT

SERVE THESE IN BURGER BUNS WITH A SELECTION OF YOUR FAVORITE RELISHES SUCH AS CORN PICKLE, JALAPENO CHILES, TOMATO CHUTNEY, OR WITH MIXED SALAD.

SERVES 4

14-ounce can chickpeas
14-ounce can kidney beans
1 red onion
1 carrot
1 zucchini
2 tablespoons oil, plus extra for
    deep-frying
½ cup (2 ounces) hazelnuts,
    finely chopped
1 tablespoon chopped fresh
    cilantro
Salt and pepper
2 eggs
All purpose flour, to dust
1 cup (3 ounces) polenta or
    yellow cornmeal

1 Drain and rinse the chickpeas and kidney beans. Place the chickpeas in a food processor and grind to a meal. Mash or finely chop the kidney beans.

2 Peel and finely chop the onion and shred the carrot and zucchini. Heat 2 tablespoons of oil in a small skillet and fry the onion until soft but not browned.

3 Tip the onion into a bowl and stir in the chickpea meal, mashed kidney beans, shredded carrot, zucchini, chopped hazelnuts, cilantro, and seasoning. Beat 1 egg and stir in to bind the ingredients together.

4 Shape the mixture into 8 burgers and dust with flour. Beat the second egg, brush it over the burgers, and coat them in the polenta. Chill for 2 hours to firm them up and allow the flavors to develop.

5 Heat about 1 inch oil in a large skillet to 350°F and fry the burgers in two batches for about 5 minutes or until golden brown, turning them over once. Serve hot with salad and relishes. Add some onion rings if you fancy a little extra.

Fried Herb Garnishes

THESE CAN BE USED TO GARNISH ALL SORTS OF DISHES AND WILL TURN A SIMPLE RECIPE INTO SOMETHING A BIT SPECIAL FOR A DINNER PARTY.

Basil or sage leaves
Sprigs of curly parsley
Oil for deep-frying

1 Choose large, unblemished basil or sage leaves and tight sprigs of parsley with fairly long stalks. Rinse and blot with paper towels until completely dry.

2 Heat 1 inch oil for frying in a deep pan to 350°F. Drop in the basil or sage leaves a few at a time and fry for about 5 seconds until they darken, become translucent, and the edges begin to curl. Drain immediately.

3 The parsley can be fried in the same way, either as individual sprigs or by tying several together with thin string and lowering the bunch into the oil.

4 Garnish your chosen dish by scattering a few basil or sage leaves over the top. The parsley can be placed in a bunch on the side of the plate or crumbled over the dish.

Vegetable Tempura with a Vinegar Dipping Sauce

ALTHOUGH NOW ONE OF JAPAN'S MOST POPULAR DISHES, TEMPURA ONLY BECAME PART OF THE NATIONAL CUISINE WHEN SIXTEENTH CENTURY PORTUGUESE SETTLERS INTRODUCED LOCAL COOKS TO DEEP-FRYING. COOK THE VEGETABLES JUST BEFORE SERVING SO THEY ARE NICELY CRISP.

SERVES 4

Dipping sauce:
6 tablespoons soy sauce
2 tablespoons rice vinegar
Small knob of ginger, peeled and cut into fine strips

Tempura:
2 pounds mixed vegetables, e.g., zucchini, broccoli florets, bell peppers, cauliflower florets, carrots, mushrooms
Oil for deep-frying
1 quantity (1½ to 2 cups) Tempura Batter (see page 14)

1 To make the dipping sauce, mix the ingredients together and pour into a serving dish.

2 For the tempura, prepare the vegetables as necessary, cutting into sticks or bite-size pieces. For firmer vegetables, such as carrots, broccoli, and cauliflower, blanch the prepared pieces in a saucepan of boiling water for 2 to 3 minutes or until almost tender.

3 Heat oil for deep-frying to 375°F. Using chopsticks or tongs, dip the vegetable pieces in the batter one at a time and drop into the oil, frying 6 to 8 pieces at a time.

4 Fry for 2 to 4 minutes until the batter is golden, then remove the vegetables from the oil and drain. Serve at once with the dipping sauce.

Thai Sweetcorn Cakes with Peanut Sauce

IF SERVING THE PEANUT SAUCE COLD, REMEMBER IT WILL THICKEN UPON STANDING SO YOU
WILL NEED TO STIR IN A FEW TABLESPOONS OF WARM WATER TO THIN IT DOWN TO THE
RIGHT CONSISTENCY.

SERVES 4 TO 6

8 snow peas
1 cup (4 ounces) sweetcorn
    kernels with peppers
1 tablespoon Thai green curry
    paste
1 tablespoon fish sauce
1 teaspoon brown sugar
1 tablespoon chopped fresh
    cilantro
¾ cup (3 ounces) all-purpose
    flour
1 egg, beaten
Oil for deep-frying

Peanut sauce:
1 small onion
1 garlic clove
1 small red chile
1 tablespoon oil
4 tablespoons crunchy peanut
    butter
2 teaspoons brown sugar
1 teaspoon fish sauce
½ cup coconut milk

To garnish:
Red chile, finely chopped
Scallions, shredded
Cilantro sprigs
Sweetcorn kernels

1 Finely chop the snow peas. In a bowl, mix together the
   sweetcorn, green curry paste, fish sauce, brown sugar,
   cilantro, and snow peas. Stir in the flour until the
   ingredients are coated and then the egg to bind
   them together.

2 To make the sauce, peel and finely chop the onion, skin and
   crush the garlic, seed and finely chop the chile. Heat the oil
   in a saucepan and fry the onion until softened. Add the
   garlic and chile and cook for 1 minute, then stir in the
   peanut butter, brown sugar, fish sauce, and coconut milk.
   Heat gently, stirring frequently so the ingredients are
   evenly combined.

3 Heat oil for deep-frying to 350°F. Drop tablespoons of
   the sweetcorn mixture into the hot oil and fry for 3 to
   4 minutes until golden brown. Drain and serve hot with the
   garnishes scattered over. Spoon a little warm peanut sauce
   on to each serving plate or serve the sauce cold as a dip,
   letting it down with warm water if it has become too thick.

Mushroom Spring Rolls

YOU CAN USE DRIED CHINESE MUSHROOMS OR ITALIAN PORCINI TO MAKE THESE CRISP ASIAN ROLLS. SOAK THE MUSHROOMS IN WATER FOR 30 MINUTES TO PLUMP THEM UP AND DRAIN WELL BEFORE ADDING TO THE FILLING. THE SOAKING WATER CAN BE KEPT AND ADDED TO SAUCES AND GRAVIES BUT STRAIN IT THROUGH A FINE STRAINER FIRST TO REMOVE ANY TINY PIECES OF GRIT FROM THE MUSHROOMS.

MAKES 12

½ ounce dried mushrooms
12 ounces brown cap
 mushrooms
½ red bell pepper
4 scallions
8 ounces cooked ham
2 tablespoons oil, plus extra for
 deep-frying
4 ounces bean sprouts
1 teaspoon fresh ginger puree
1 tablespoon rice vinegar
2 tablespoons dark soy sauce
1 teaspoon sesame oil
1 tablespoon cornstarch
12 spring roll wrappers

1 Place the dried mushrooms in a bowl, pour over boiling water to cover, and set aside to soak for 30 minutes. Drain the mushrooms and chop any large pieces.

2 Finely chop the brown cap mushrooms, seed and finely chop the pepper, chop the scallions, and finely chop the ham.

3 Heat 2 tablespoons of oil in a skillet, add the brown cap mushrooms, pepper, and scallions and fry for 5 minutes. Stir in the dried mushrooms, ham, beansprouts, ginger puree, rice vinegar, soy sauce, and sesame oil and cook for 2 minutes. Set aside to cool.

4 In a small bowl, mix the cornstarch with 4 tablespoons cold water until smooth. Divide the mushroom filling between the spring roll wrappers, brush the edges of the wrappers with the cornstarch mix and roll up around the filling, tucking in the sides and pressing the edges together to seal.

5 Heat oil for deep-frying to 350°F and deep-fry the rolls for 4 to 5 minutes until golden brown. Drain and serve with a small bowl of dark soy sauce for dipping.

6 | just potatoes

The world's favorite snack has to be the ubiquitous French fry.

Thin and stringy, short and fat, matchstick cut, or traditional

thick-cut fries, a bag of these must satisfy more hungry appetites

than any other food. Few people would argue that the humble

potato is just made for deep-frying and whichever way you do it the

results are equally delicious.

English Chip-shop Fries ILLUSTRATED ABOVE

THE TRADITIONAL ACCOMPANIMENT TO THAT GREAT BRITISH FAVORITE, BATTERED FISH. IN THE UK THE FRENCH FRIES WOULD BE SERVED IN NEWSPAPER ALONGSIDE THE FISH, LIBERALLY SPRINKLED WITH SALT AND MALT VINEGAR.

SERVES 4

8 medium (2 pounds) Idaho potatoes
Oil for deep-frying
Salt
Malt vinegar

1 Peel and cut the potatoes into roughly ½ x 2½–inch batons. Rinse, drain, and pat dry with paper towels.

2 Heat oil for deep-frying to 325 °F, place half the batons in a frying basket and lower carefully into the hot oil. Fry for 5 minutes until they are soft but still pale-colored. Drain and blanch the remaining batons in the same way.

3 When ready to serve, reheat the oil to 375 °F. Return all the fries to the basket and fry for 3 to 4 minutes until crisp and golden, shaking the basket occasionally.

4 Drain, sprinkle with salt and malt vinegar and serve at once.

Buffalo Fries ILLUSTRATED LEFT

MAKE AS FOR ENGLISH CHIP-SHOP FRIES BUT SCRUB THE POTATOES WELL AND LEAVE THE PEEL ON.

French Fries

THE ULTIMATE COMFORT FOOD! SERVE WITH BURGERS, SAUSAGES, AND STEAKS, WITH MUSTARD OR KETCHUP, OR BEST OF ALL, ON THEIR OWN—CRISP, GOLDEN, AND PIPING HOT.

SERVES 4

8 large (2 pounds) Idaho
    potatoes
Oil for deep-frying
Salt

1 Peel and cut the potatoes into roughly ¼ x 2½–inch batons. Rinse, drain, and pat dry with paper towels.

2 Heat oil for deep-frying to 325°F, place half the fries in a frying basket, and lower carefully into the hot oil. Fry for 5 minutes until the fries are soft but still pale-colored. Drain and blanch the remaining fries in the same way.

3 When ready to serve, reheat the oil to 375°F. Return all the fries to the basket and fry for 2 minutes until crisp and golden, shaking the basket occasionally.

4 Drain, sprinkle with salt, and serve at once.

TIPS FOR PERFECT FRIES:

- When deep-frying potatoes, choose Idaho potatoes.

- Rinse the potatoes after you have cut them into French fries or soak in a bowl of cold water to remove excess starch—this stops them sticking together in the frying basket.

- Prepare them ahead and soak in a bowl of salted water so they are crisper when cooked. Drain and pat dry thoroughly before frying.

- If you don't have a cooking thermometer, drop a fry into the hot oil and if it sinks and doesn't move the oil is not hot enough. The oil is ready when it floats and the oil bubbles around it.

Straw Potato Fries

CUT THE POTATOES INTO FINE JULIENNE STRIPS USING A SHARP KNIFE OR SAVE TIME BY PUSHING THEM THROUGH THE SHREDDING ATTACHMENT OF A FOOD PROCESSOR.

SERVES 4

4 medium (1 pound) Idaho
   potatoes
Oil for deep-frying
Salt

1 Peel and cut the potatoes into fine julienne strips. Wash, drain, and dry thoroughly.

2 Heat oil for deep-frying to 375°F and fry the strips in small batches for 2 to 3 minutes until golden brown and crisp, shaking the basket or turning them over from time to time.

3 Drain, sprinkle with salt, and serve with broiled meat and fish.

Matchstick Fries   ILLUSTRATED BELOW

KNOWN AS "POMMES ALLUMETTES" (MATCHSTICK POTATOES) IN FRANCE. CUT THE POTATOES INTO SLIGHTLY LARGER STRIPS THAN FOR THE STRAW POTATO FRIES—¼ X 2½ INCHES—AND DEEP-FRY IN THE SAME WAY FOR 5 MINUTES OR UNTIL GOLDEN BROWN.

Game Fries ILLUSTRATED ABOVE

SERVE AS AN ACCOMPANIMENT TO ROAST PHEASANT AND OTHER GAME BIRDS OR TO NIBBLE
WITH PRE-DINNER DRINKS

SERVES 4

**4 medium-sized (1 pound) Idaho
    potatoes
Oil for deep-frying
Salt**

1 Peel the potatoes (or leave unpeeled, as preferred) and cut
crossways into wafer thin slices. Immediately place in a bowl
of cold water and leave to soak for 15 minutes to remove
excess starch. Drain and dry thoroughly.

2 Heat oil for deep-frying to 375°F and fry the potato slices in
small quantities for 2 minutes until crisp and golden brown,
shaking the basket occasionally or turning the slices over.

3 Drain, sprinkle with salt, and serve.

Lattice Fries ILLUSTRATED LEFT

MAKE AS FOR GAME FRIES BUT CUT THE POTATO SLICES WITH A
FLUTED VEGETABLE SLICER TO GIVE A HONEYCOMB EFFECT.

Skins with Guacamole Dip

WHEN SCOOPING OUT THE POTATO FLESH, LEAVE A ¼-INCH LAYER OF POTATO AROUND THE EDGE SO THE SKINS DON'T COLLAPSE, AND TAKE CARE NOT TO SPLIT THE SKIN WITH THE SPOON.

SERVES 4

Guacamole dip:
2 medium tomatoes
½ small onion
1 to 2 green or red chile
     peppers
1 tablespoon fresh lime juice
Salt and pepper
2 ripe avocados
1 tablespoon chopped fresh
     parsley or cilantro

Skin:
4 large Idaho potatoes
Oil for deep-frying

1 For the guacamole, finely chop the tomatoes, peel and finely chop or shred the onion, and seed and finely chop the chile peppers. Mix the tomatoes, onion, chiles, and lime juice in a bowl and season with salt and pepper. Cover and set aside for 1 to 2 hours to allow the flavors to develop. Prepare the avocados for the dip no more than 30 minutes before serving or they will start to turn brown.

2 Score the potatoes around the center with the point of a sharp knife. Bake in a preheated 400°F oven for 50 minutes to 1 hour or microwave for 20 minutes on full power until the potatoes are tender when pierced with a skewer.

3 Leave the potatoes until cool enough to handle, cut them in half, and scoop out the flesh with a spoon. Cut the skins into fat wedges with a sharp knife.

4 Halve the avocados, remove the pits, and scoop the flesh into a bowl, discarding the skins. Coarsely mash with a fork and then mix into the tomato mixture. Sprinkle on some fresh parsley or cilantro as a garnish.

5 Heat oil for deep-frying to 375°F and fry the potato wedges for about 5 minutes until golden brown and crisp. Drain and serve with the guacamole.

Bubble and Squeak Cakes Illustrated left

CHOOSE A CABBAGE WITH DEEP GREEN LEAVES TO GIVE A GOOD COLOR CONTRAST. SERVE THE CAKES ON THEIR OWN WITH BROWN SAUCE OR KETCHUP OR AS AN ACCOMPANIMENT.

SERVES 4

4 medium (1 pound) boiling
   potatoes, e.g., round white
1 medium carrot
4 ounces dark green cabbage
   leaves with coarse stalks
   removed
4 scallions
2 bacon slices
1 tablespoon oil plus, extra for
   deep-frying
4 tablespoons hot milk
Salt, pepper, and nutmeg
All-purpose flour, to dust
1 egg, beaten
8 tablespoons dry breadcrumbs

1 Peel the potatoes, cut into chunks, and cook in a saucepan of boiling water until tender.

2 Meanwhile, peel and shred the carrot, finely shred the cabbage leaves, finely chop the scallions, and chop the bacon slices.

3 Heat 1 tablespoon of oil in a saucepan, add the bacon and cook until lightly browned. Add the carrot, cabbage, and scallions, cover the pan and cook over a gentle heat for 3 to 4 minutes or until the cabbage is tender.

4 Drain the potatoes and mash with the hot milk. Stir in the bacon and cabbage mixture and season with salt, pepper, and a pinch of nutmeg. Leave to cool before shaping into 8 round, flat cakes. Dust the cakes with flour, brush with beaten egg, and coat with breadcrumbs. Chill for 1 hour.

5 Heat about 1 inch of oil in a large skillet to 350°F and deep-fry the cakes for about 5 minutes until golden, turning once. Drain and serve.

Almond Potato Bites

CRISP, NUTTY, AND CRUNCHY, THESE COULD BE SERVED WITH ROAST CHICKEN, BROILED PORK CHOPS, OR BRAISED BEEF. CHOPPED HAZELNUTS OR PEANUTS CAN ALSO BE USED.

SERVES 4

6 medium (1½ pounds) boiling
   potatoes, e.g., round white
2 ounces (½ stick) butter
Salt and pepper
2 egg yolks
All-purpose flour, to dust
1 egg, beaten
¾ cup (3 ounces) almonds, finely
   chopped
Oil for deep-frying

1 Peel the potatoes and cook in a pan of boiling water until tender. Drain and mash with the butter and seasoning.

2 Return the mash to the saucepan over a gentle heat, add the egg yolks, and stir until the mixture leaves the bottom of the pan clean. Leave to cool.

3 Roll into golf ball-size balls and dust with flour. Brush with beaten egg and coat in the chopped almonds. Chill for 1 hour.

4 Heat oil for deep-frying to 350°F and deep-fry in batches for 4 to 5 minutes until golden brown. Drain and serve.

Spiced New Potatoes

CHOOSE SMALL, EVEN-SIZED NEW POTATOES AND LEAVE THEIR SKINS ON. STEAM OR COOK IN A SAUCEPAN OF BOILING WATER UNTIL TENDER BEFORE COATING IN THE SPICE MIXTURE.

SERVES 4

1 egg white
½ teaspoon hot chili powder
1 teaspoon ground coriander
½ teaspoon turmeric
½ cup (2 ounces) all-purpose
    flour
¼ cup (2 fluid ounces) water
Salt and pepper
1 cup (3 ounces) dry
    breadcrumbs
1½ pounds small new potatoes,
    cooked
Oil for deep-frying
1 teaspoon dried mint

Curried mayonnaise:
8 tablespoons mayonnaise
2 teaspoons curry paste

1 In a bowl, whisk the egg white until frothy, then whisk in the chili powder, coriander, turmeric, flour, water, salt, and pepper.

2 Mix the breadcrumbs and oregano together. Dip the potatoes in the spicy batter, and coat with the crumb mixture.

3 Heat oil for deep-frying to 375 °F and deep-fry the potatoes for 3 to 4 minutes until crisp and golden brown. Drain.

4 Stir the mayonnaise and curry paste together and serve with the hot potatoes. Garnish with mint.

Potato and Parsnip Rolls

A HANDY WAY TO USE UP LEFT-OVER BOILED POTATOES AND PARSNIPS, THE ROLLS CAN BE MADE AHEAD AND FROZEN UNTIL NEEDED.

SERVES 4

3 medium (12 ounces) boiling
   potatoes, e.g, round white
9 ounces parsnips
2 ounces (½ stick) butter
2 egg yolks
½ cup (2 ounces) shredded
   Cheddar cheese
1 teaspoon fresh thyme leaves
1 tablespoon chopped parsley
Salt and paprika
All-purpose flour, to dust
1 egg, beaten
⅔ cup (3 ounces) dry
   breadcrumbs
Oil for deep-frying

1 Peel the potatoes and parsnips and cut into even-size pieces. Cook in a saucepan of boiling water until tender, drain and mash with the butter.

2 Return the mash to the saucepan over a gentle heat, stir in the egg yolks and continue stirring until the mash leaves the bottom of the saucepan clean. Remove from the heat and stir in the thyme, parsley, salt, and paprika to taste. Leave to cool.

3 Mold the potato mixture into cork shapes, dust with flour, brush with beaten egg, and coat in the breadcrumbs. Chill for 1 hour.

4 Heat oil for deep-frying to 350°F and deep-fry the rolls for 4 to 5 minutes until golden brown. Drain and serve.

Souffle Potatoes

THESE LIGHT POTATO PUFFS NEED TO BE BLANCHED FIRST AND THEN RE-FRIED AT A HIGHER TEMPERATURE TO MAKE THEM GOLDEN AND CRISP.

SERVES 4

4 medium (1 pound) Idaho
   potatoes
Oil for deep-frying
Salt

1 Peel the potatoes and cut into very thin slices, about ⅛-inch thick. Pat the slices dry with paper towels but don't soak them in cold water or rinse them as the starch is needed to help them puff up.

2 Heat oil for deep-frying to 300°F and fry the slices in small batches, as the starch will make them stick together. Fry each batch for 1 to 2 minutes, shaking the frying basket gently, until the slices begin to swell.

3 Drain and set aside until ready to serve—the puffed slices will sink back down but this is normal.

4 Reheat oil to 375°F, put the slices back in the frying basket and plunge into the hot oil. Fry for 1 to 2 minutes or until puffed and golden brown. Drain and sprinkle with salt.

Pommes Dauphine

POPULAR IN FRANCE, THESE LIGHT, FLUFFY POTATO CROQUETTES ARE A MIX OF MASH AND CHOUX PASTE (A DOUGH USED FOR MAKING PROFITEROLES). SERVE THEM AS AN ACCOMPANIMENT TO PLAINLY BROILED CHICKEN OR PORK WITH A CREAMY RED BELL PEPPER SAUCE.

SERVES 4

Red bell pepper sauce:
1 garlic clove
1 red bell pepper
1 tablespoon oil
1 teaspoon sweet chilli sauce
14-ounce can chopped tomatoes
1 teaspoon sugar
½ cup (4 fluid ounces) light
    cream

Potatoes:
4 medium (1 pound) boiling
    potatoes, e.g., round white
4 ounces (1 stick) butter
Salt and pepper
⅔ cup (6 fluid ounces) water
1 cup all-purpose flour
2 medium eggs, beaten
Oil for deep-frying
Snipped chives, to garnish

1 To make the sauce, peel and crush the garlic, seed, and chop the pepper.

2 Heat the oil in a saucepan and fry the garlic and pepper until softened. Add the chili sauce, tomatoes, and sugar, cover the pan and simmer for 30 minutes. Blend the ingredients to create a sauce and stir in the cream.

3 For the potatoes, peel, cut into chunks, and cook in a saucepan of boiling water until tender. Drain, mash with half the butter, and season with salt and pepper.

4 Cut up the rest of the butter into small pieces and place in a saucepan with the water. Heat until the butter melts, then bring to a fast boil. Remove the pan from the heat, tip in all the flour, and beat with a wooden spoon until the mixture forms a smooth ball that leaves the sides of the pan.

5 Cool slightly, then beat in the eggs a little at a time. Stir this mixture into the potato mash and leave to cool.

6 Heat oil for deep-frying to 325°F. Using two large spoons, scoop the mixture into egg-shaped croquettes and drop into the hot oil. Fry for 4 to 5 minutes until golden brown. Drain and serve with the warmed sauce and snipped chives sprinkled over.

Sweet Potato Fritters with Tomato Salsa

ADD EXTRA CHILE TO THE SALSA IF YOU LIKE THINGS HOT. THE FRITTERS CAN ALSO BE SERVED AS AN ACCOMPANIMENT TO BROILED MEATS AND FISH.

SERVES 4 TO 6

Fritters:

6 small to medium (1½ pounds) sweet potatoes
1 onion
2 garlic cloves
½ red bell pepper
2 tablespoons oil, plus extra for deep-frying
1 tablespoon chopped fresh parsley
All-purpose flour, to dust
1 egg, beaten
⅔ cup (2 ounces) fresh whole grain breadcrumbs

Salsa:

3 medium (12 ounces) tomatoes
2 sticks of celery
3 scallions
1 red chile
1 tablespoon chopped fresh mint
2 tablespoons white wine vinegar

1 To make the fritters, peel the sweet potatoes, boil, and mash. Peel and finely chop the onion, peel and crush the garlic, seed and finely chop the pepper.

2 Heat 2 tablespoons of oil in a skillet and cook the onion until soft. Add the garlic and pepper and fry for 2 to 3 minutes. Stir in the parsley, mix into the sweet potato mash, and leave to cool.

3 Shape the mixture into small balls. Dust with flour, coat in the beaten egg, and roll in the breadcrumbs. Chill for 1 hour to firm up.

4 To make the salsa, peel, seed, and chop the tomatoes, finely chop the celery, trim and slice the scallions, seed, and finely chop the chile. Mix the tomatoes, celery, onions, and chile with the mint and vinegar and chill until ready to serve.

5 Heat oil for deep-frying to 375°F and fry the fritters in batches for 2 to 3 minutes until golden brown. Drain and serve hot with the salsa.

7 doughnuts & other sweet treats

Doughnuts are the favorite childhood treat that every grownup loves as well. The perfect doughnut should be light and spongy with a crisp white sugar coating and if they're good one will never be enough. America is the doughnut capital of the world but variations on the traditional jam-filled or iced ring doughnut pop up in many other countries. The Spaniards dip finger-shaped churros into mugs of rich hot chocolate, the Greeks enjoy loukomathes scooped into paper cones and drenched with honey. If you have a sweet tooth, you'll find plenty to tempt you in this chapter.

Cannoli

THESE CRISP PASTRY TUBES FILLED WITH RICOTTA CHEESE AND CANDIED FRUITS ARE A SICILIAN SPECIALITY WHERE THEY TAKE PRIDE OF PLACE IN THE LOCAL CAKE SHOPS. CANNOLI MOLDS CAN BE BOUGHT FROM KITCHENWARE STORES OR ASK AT YOUR LOCAL HARDWARE SHOP FOR FOUR PIECES OF STAINLESS STEEL TUBING, AROUND 6 INCHES LONG AND ¾-INCH IN DIAMETER. IN SICILY, COOKS WOULD PROBABLY USE OLIVE OIL TO FRY THE PASTRY BUT OTHER LESS FLAVORED OILS SUCH AS PALM OR VEGETABLE WORK EQUALLY WELL.

MAKES 16

Pastry:

1¼ cups (6 ounces) all-purpose flour

¼ teaspoon salt

2 ounces (½ stick) butter

Scant ¼ cup (1½ ounce) superfine sugar

1 egg, beaten

2 to 3 tablespoons white wine or dry Marsala, to mix

1 egg white, lightly beaten

Oil for deep-frying

Filling:

2 ounces dark chocolate

1¼ cups (12 ounces) ricotta

¼ cup (2 ounces) confectioners' sugar

Rind of 1 orange, finely shredded

⅓ cup (2 ounces) chopped glacé fruits, e.g., candied citrus peel

Extra confectioners' sugar, to dust

1 To make the pastry, sift the flour and salt into a bowl and rub in the butter until like fine breadcrumbs. Stir in the sugar, then mix in the egg and enough wine or Marsala to make soft but not sticky dough. Knead until smooth and roll out thinly on a floured surface.

2 Cut the pastry into 16 squares, roughly 3 inches in size. Dust four metal cannoli tubes with flour and wrap a pastry square loosely around each on the diagonal, brushing the edges with egg white and pressing together to seal.

3 Heat oil for deep-frying to 350°F and deep-fry for 3 to 4 minutes or until the pastry is golden and crisp. Drain and when cool enough to handle, rotate the metal tubes gently so you can pull them out of the pastry. Cook three more batches of pastry tubes in the same way.

4 To make the filling, very finely chop or shred the chocolate and mix with the cheese, icing sugar, orange rind, and candied fruits. When the pastry tubes are cold, pipe or spoon the filling into them. Dust with confectioners' sugar and eat on the day they are made.

Basic Doughnut Dough

IT IS ESPECIALLY IMPORTANT TO HEAT THE OIL TO THE CORRECT TEMPERATURE WHEN FRYING DOUGHNUTS. TOO COOL AND THEY WILL ABSORB TOO MUCH OIL, BECOMING HEAVY AND FATTY INSTEAD OF LIGHT AND CRISP, TOO HOT AND THE OUTSIDE OF THE DOUGHNUTS WILL BURN WHILE THE CENTERS STAY STICKY AND UNDER-DONE. DOUGHNUTS ARE BEST EATEN ON THE DAY THEY ARE MADE.

4 cups (1 pound) self-rising
    flour
1 tablespoon baking powder
¾ cup (3 ounces) superfine
    sugar
2 eggs
1 cup (8 fluid ounces) milk
2 ounces (½ stick) butter,
    melted and cooled

1 Sift the flour and baking powder into a mixing bowl and stir in superfine sugar.

2 Beat together the eggs, milk, and melted butter, add to the dry ingredients and mix to a soft dough. Cover the bowl and chill for 1 hour to firm up the dough.

Plain Sugar-dusted Doughnuts   ILLUSTRATED RIGHT

ADD A FESTIVE TOUCH BY MIXING THE DUSTING SUGAR WITH A LITTLE POWDERED FOOD COLORING. PUT THE SUGAR AND COLORING INTO A SMALL PLASTIC BAG, TWIST THE TOP TO SEAL AND SHAKE WELL.

MAKES 12

1 quantity of Basic Doughnut
    Dough (see above)
Oil for deep-frying
Superfine sugar, to dust

1 Make up the dough as directed. Divide it into 12 pieces and roll into balls.

2 Heat oil for deep-frying to 350°F and fry the doughnuts in batches for about 8–10 minutes or until puffed and golden brown.

3 Drain, sprinkle generously with superfine sugar, and leave to cool before serving.

Ring Doughnuts with Vanilla and Chocolate Frosting

RATHER THAN WASTING THE THE CUT-OUT CENTERS, THEY CAN BE TURNED INTO MINI DOUGHNUT BITES WITH MAPLE SYRUP AND STRAWBERRIES.

MAKES ABOUT 16

4 cups (1 pound) self-rising
   flour
1 tablespoon baking powder
½ teaspoon ground cinnamon
¾ cup (3 ounces) granulated
   sugar
2 eggs
1 cup (8 fluid ounces) milk
2 ounces (½ stick) butter,
   melted
Oil for deep-frying

Frosting:
Superfine sugar, to dust
2½ cups (12 ounces)
   confectioners' sugar
Few drops of vanilla
1 tablespoon cocoa powder
Chocolate vermicelli
Hundreds and thousands

1 Sift the self-rising flour, baking powder, and cinnamon into a mixing bowl and stir in the sugar.

2 Beat together the eggs, milk, and melted butter, add to the dry ingredients, and mix to a soft dough. Cover the bowl and chill for 1 hour to firm up the dough.

3 Roll out the dough on a floured surface about ½–inch thick. Flour a 3-inch plain pastry cutter and stamp out rounds. Cut holes out of the center of each round with a floured 1-inch cutter. Fry the centers as mini-doughnuts or re-roll with the other dough trimmings and make more rings.

4 Heat 1½ inches oil for frying in a wide heavy-bottomed pan to 350°F. Fry the doughnuts two or three at a time for about 5 minutes until golden, turning over once or twice. Drain, sprinkle with a little superfine sugar, and leave to cool.

5 Sift half the confectioners' sugar into a bowl, add the vanilla and enough cold water to mix to a smooth frosting.

6 Sift the rest of the confectioners' sugar with the cocoa powder into another bowl and mix in cold water to make a smooth frosting.

7 Spread the top of half the doughnuts with the vanilla frosting and the rest with the chocolate frosting. Sprinkle with chocolate vermicelli and hundreds and thousands. Leave to set.

Gulab Jamun

A STYLISH INDIAN DESSERT THAT WOULD MAKE A FITTING FINALE TO A DINNER PARTY OF CURRIED OR SPICY DISHES. LEAVE THE CRISP-FRIED DOUGH BALLS TO COOL IN THE ROSEWATER SYRUP SO THEY BECOME SOFT AND SPONGY AND SERVE IN INDIVIDUAL BOWLS WITH A FEW ROSE PETALS FOR DECORATION. DO NOT USE PETALS FROM A ROSE BOUGHT AT A FLORIST BECAUSE THEY ARE LIKELY TO HAVE BEEN SPRAYED WITH CHEMICALS.

SERVES 4

1 cup (4 ounces) all-purpose
    flour
½ teaspoon baking powder
6 tablespoons milk powder
2 ounces (½ stick) butter
About 4 tablespoons milk
Oil for deep-frying

Syrup:
1 cup (8 ounces) confectioners
    sugar
4 tablespoons water
1 tablespoon rose water

To serve:
Rose petals

1 Sift the flour, baking powder, and milk powder into a bowl. Rub in the butter until the mixture is like breadcrumbs and add enough milk to mix to an elastic dough.

2 Divide the dough into 16 pieces and roll into balls.

3 Heat oil for deep-frying to 350°F and fry the balls in batches for 4 to 5 minutes or until golden brown. Drain the balls as they cook and then transfer in a large heatproof bowl.

4 To make the syrup, heat the sugar and water in a pan until the sugar dissolves. Bring to a boil and simmer for 1 minute. Stir in the rose water and pour the hot syrup over the dough balls. Leave to cool.

5 To serve, wash and dry the rose petals. Divide the dough balls and syrup between individual serving dishes and float a few rose petals on each.

Traditional Jam Doughnuts

SEAL THE JAM TIGHTLY INSIDE THE DOUGH OR IT WILL LEAK OUT DURING FRYING. YOU CAN USE YOUR FAVORITE JAM TO FILL THE DOUGHNUTS BUT THOSE WITH A STRONG FRUIT FLAVOR SUCH AS RASPBERRY, STRAWBERRY, APRICOT, OR BLACKBERRY WORK THE BEST.

MAKES 12

1 quantity of Basic Doughnut
    Dough (see page 132)
About 2 tablespoons jam
1 egg white, lightly beaten
Oil for deep-frying
Superfine sugar, to dust

1 Make up the dough. Roll out about ½-inch thick and cut out 2½-inch rounds using a plain cutter, gathering up and re-rolling the trimmings until you have 24 rounds.

2 Spoon a little jam into the center of 12 of the rounds. Brush the edges with lightly beaten egg white and press the remaining rounds on top, pressing and pinching the edges together to make a tight seal.

3 Heat oil for deep-frying to 350°F and fry the doughnuts in batches for about 10 minutes until golden brown, turning them over occasionally so they color evenly. Drain, sprinkle with superfine sugar, and leave to cool.

Apple Doughnut Parcels

SERVE THESE JUST WARM AS A DELICIOUS DESSERT WITH PLENTY OF WHIPPED CREAM OR
VANILLA ICE CREAM.

MAKES 12

2 medium-sized tart apples,
    e.g., Baldwin, Cortland
2 tablespoons golden raisins
2 tablespoons orange juice
Granulated sugar, to taste
1 quantity of Basic Doughnut
    Dough (see page 132)
1 egg white, lightly beaten
Oil for deep-frying
Superfine sugar and ground
    cinnamon, to dust

1 Peel, core, and chop the apples. Place in a non-stick
saucepan with the golden raisins and orange juice, cover
and simmer gently until the apples are soft but not falling
apart. Add sugar to taste and leave to cool.

2 Make up the dough and roll out about ½-inch thick. Dust a
sharp knife with flour and cut out 3-inch squares of dough,
gathering up and re-rolling the trimmings as necessary until
you have 12 squares.

3 Drain any excess liquid from the apple mixture and spoon a
little on one side of each dough square. Brush the edges of
the squares with egg white and fold one corner over the
filling to meet the opposite corner to make a triangular-
shaped parcel, pinching the edges together to seal.

4 Heat oil for deep-frying to 350°F and fry the doughnut
parcels in batches for about 5 minutes, turning them over
occasionally, until golden brown. Drain and dust with a
mix of superfine sugar and ground cinnamon—add about
½ teaspoon cinnamon to 3 tablespoons sugar.

Loukoumathes

THESE SMALL STICKY DOUGHNUTS ARE POPULAR IN GREECE WHERE THEY ARE EATEN AS AN ACCOMPANIMENT TO THE THICK, SEMI-SWEET GREEK COFFEE CALLED METRIO. AFTER FRYING, DRIZZLE THE DOUGHNUTS WITH SYRUP AND DUST WITH CINNAMON BEFORE SERVING.

SERVES 6

3 cups (12 ounces) all-purpose
  flour
1 teaspoon sugar
Pinch of salt
¼–ounce packet of instant dried
  yeast
1 cup (8 fluid ounces) lukewarm
  water
Oil for deep-frying

Syrup:
½ cup (4 fluid ounces) runny
  honey
2 tablespoons lemon juice

To serve:
Ground cinnamon

1 Sift the flour into a bowl and stir in the sugar, salt, and yeast. Make a well in the center, pour in the water, and mix to a soft dough. Knead on a floured surface until smooth. Transfer to a lightly oiled plastic bag, seal the top, and leave in a warm place until the dough doubles in size.

2 Split open the bag, and with your fingers pinch off small walnut-sized pieces of dough on to a plate.

3 Heat oil for deep-frying to 350°F and cook the dough balls in batches for about 5 to 6 minutes until deep golden brown, turning them over as they cook so they brown evenly. Drain.

4 For the syrup, warm the honey and lemon juice in a saucepan and drizzle over the hot doughnuts. Dust with ground cinnamon and serve warm.

Caramelized Walnuts

SERVE THESE WITH AFTER-DINNER COFFEE AS A DELICIOUS ALTERNATIVE TO CHOCOLATES OR
PETITS FOURS. BLANCHING THE WALNUTS BEFORE FRYING REMOVES ANY BITTER FLAVOR THEY
MIGHT HAVE.

SERVES 6

2 cups (9 ounces) walnut halves
⅓ cup (3 ounces) honey
1 tablespoon lemon juice
¾ cup (6 ounces) superfine
**   sugar**
Oil for deep-frying
4 tablespoons sesame seeds

1 Simmer the walnut halves in a pan of boiling water for
2 minutes. Drain and dry with paper towels.

2 In a bowl, mix together the honey and lemon juice, add the
walnuts, and stir until coated. Set aside for 2 to 3 hours,
stirring occasionally.

3 Spread out the superfine sugar on a plate, drain the
walnuts, and coat them in the sugar.

4 Heat oil for deep-frying to 350°F. Fry the walnuts in two
batches for about 2 minutes each until just golden—don't
let the oil get too hot or the walnuts color too much or they
will taste burnt and bitter.

5 Drain the walnuts on a sheet of waxed paper and sprinkle
with the sesame seeds. Serve warm or cold.

Creamy Chocolate Phyllos

SERVE THESE HOT SO THAT WHEN YOU BREAK INTO THE CRISP PHYLLO SHELL, THE CREAMY DARK CHOCOLATE CENTER OOZES OUT. SERVE THEM ON THEIR OWN OR WITH ICE CREAM.

MAKES 12

4 ounces white almond paste
6 tablespoons (3 ounces) cream cheese
1 teaspoon lemon rind, finely shredded
1 teaspoon lemon juice
2 teaspoons all-purpose flour
6 sheets of phyllo pastry, measuring 7 x 12 inches
12 small squares of dark chocolate
1 egg white, lightly beaten
Oil for deep-frying

1 Finely chop the almond paste and place in a bowl. Stir in the cream cheese, lemon rind, juice, and flour until evenly combined. Chill the mixture for 1 hour.

2 Cut the phyllo sheets in half lengthways to give 12 long strips. Spoon a little of the almond mixture at the end of one strip and place a square of chocolate on top. Fold the corner of the pastry diagonally over the filling and continue folding up the strip to make a triangular parcel. Dab a little egg white on the top edges of the pastry and press them together to seal.

3 Repeat with the remaining phyllo strips and filling to make 12 parcels. Heat oil for deep-frying to 350°F and fry the parcels for 2 to 3 minutes until golden brown and crisp. Drain and serve warm.

Churros

IN SPAIN THESE SMALL, FINGER-SHAPED DOUGHNUTS ARE EATEN AS AN ACCOMPANIMENT TO THICK, CREAMY HOT CHOCOLATE.

SERVES 4

1½ cups (6 ounces) all-purpose flour
Pinch of salt
1 cup (8 fluid ounces) water
1 egg, beaten
Oil for deep-frying
Superfine sugar, to dust

1 Sift the flour and salt together on to a plate. Bring the water to a fast boil and tip in all the flour. Remove the pan from the heat and beat vigorously with a wooden spoon until the dough forms a ball and leaves the sides of the pan clean.

2 Gradually beat in the egg until the mixture is smooth, shiny, and holds its shape.

3 Spoon the mixture into a piping bag fitted with a large star nozzle, pushing it in firmly so there are no air bubbles. Heat oil for deep-frying to 350°F and pipe 3 to 4-inch lengths into the oil, cutting off each length with a knife and letting it fall gently into the oil.

4 Fry the churros in batches until golden brown, for about 2 to 3 minutes. Drain, dredge with superfine sugar, and eat while still warm—if left to go cold they will become tough and chewy.

8 | fruity desserts

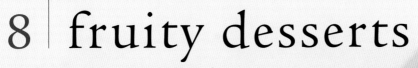

Deep-fried fruit is unbeatable if you want a truly satisfying

dessert. When it comes to rounding off a great Chinese

meal, top of everyone's list is sesame toffee fritters.

Phyllo pastry fries to a deliciously crisp shell and can

be wrapped around any number of fruit fillings. Tangy

sauces made with sharper-flavored fruits such as

raspberries or blueberries make excellent accompaniments

to plain fritters or beignets. Flavor the fritters

with spices like cinnamon or

ginger and serve.

Tropical Fruit Salad with Gingered French Toast ILLUSTRATED LEFT

ANY COMBINATION OF TROPICAL FRUITS CAN BE USED, SUCH AS MANGO, PAPAYA, PINEAPPLE, BANANA, STAR FRUIT, AND LYCHEES. SERVE WITH WHIPPED CREAM OR SOUR CREAM.

SERVES 6

2 pounds mixed tropical fruits
6 tablespoons fresh pineapple juice
2 tablespoons rum, optional

French toast:
3 eggs
½ cup (4 fluid ounces) milk
2 tablespoons superfine sugar
1 teaspoon ground ginger
6 large slices of thick-cut white bread
Oil for deep-frying
Confectioners' sugar, to dust

1 Prepare the fruit as necessary and cut into bite-sized pieces. Place in a bowl, spoon over the pineapple juice and rum (if using), and chill in the refrigerator until ready to serve.

2 To make the French toast, whisk together the eggs, milk, sugar, and ginger in a shallow dish. Cut each slice of bread into two or four triangles.

3 Heat oil for deep-frying to 350°F. Dip the bread in the egg mixture until well coated and fry in batches for 1 to 2 minutes until golden brown. Drain, dust with confectioners' sugar, and serve hot with the fruit salad.

Cherry Almond Phyllos

IF USING CANNED OR BOTTLED CHERRIES, DRAIN THEM THOROUGHLY AND PAT DRY WITH A PAPER TOWEL SO EXCESS JUICE DOESN'T SEEP INTO THE PASTRY.

SERVES 6

6 tablespoons cream cheese
1 cup (3½ ounces) ground almonds
¼ cup (2 ounces) soft light brown sugar
1½ cups (8 ounces) pitted cherries
6 sheets of phyllo pastry, measuring 12 x 7 inches
Oil for brushing and deep-frying
Confectioners' sugar, to dredge

1 In a bowl, mix together the cream cheese, ground almonds, and sugar. Roughly chop the cherries and stir in.

2 Place a sheet of phyllo on a board and spoon one-sixth of the mixture down the center. Brush the pastry edges with oil and roll it around the filling, tucking in the sides to make a log shape. Repeat with the rest of the phyllo and filling to make six parcels.

3 Heat oil for deep-frying to 325°F and deep-fry the parcels in two batches for 3 to 4 minutes each until golden. Drain and dredge with confectioners' sugar before serving warm with whipped cream or vanilla ice cream.

Chinese Toffee Fruit Fritters

WHEN MAKING THE TOFFEE, ENSURE THE SUGAR DISSOLVES COMPLETELY BEFORE YOU BRING IT TO A BOIL OR YOU WILL HAVE AN UNPLEASANTLY GRANULAR CARAMEL.

SERVES 4

1 cup (4 ounces) all-purpose flour, plus extra for dusting
2 teaspoons vegetable oil, plus extra for deep-frying
1 tart dessert apple, e.g., Baldwin, Cortland
2 pineapple rings
1 medium banana
Sesame oil for greasing
Ice cubes
1¾ cups (12 ounces) granulated sugar
3 tablespoons mixed black and white sesame seeds

1 Sift the flour into a bowl, stir in about ⅝ cup cold water to make a smooth batter and then stir in 2 teaspoons vegetable oil. Leave to stand for 30 minutes.

2 Peel and core the apples and cut each one into eight wedges. Cut each pineapple ring into quarters, peel and cut the banana into four chunks.

3 Heat oil for deep-frying to 375°F. Dust the fruit with flour and drop about six pieces into the batter. Lift them out one at a time with a slotted spoon and carefully place in the oil—adding the fruit pieces one at a time prevents them sticking together as they fry.

4 Fry for 2 to 3 minutes until golden, remove and drain on paper towels. Fry the remaining fruit in the same way.

5 Oil a large plate with a little sesame oil and have ready a bowl filled with cold water and ice cubes.

6 To make the caramel, heat the granulated sugar in a heavy-bottomed pan with ¾ cup (6 fluid ounces) water until the sugar dissolves. Bring to a boil and boil until the syrup caramelizes to a rich golden brown. Remove the pan from the heat and add the sesame seeds and fruit pieces, tossing until coated with the caramel.

7 Turn out at once on to the oiled plate and, using two forks, dip the pieces one at a time into the iced water to set the toffee coating. Serve hot.

Apple Fritter Rings with Apricot Sauce

USE FIRM DESSERT APPLES RATHER THAN COOKING APPLES THAT WILL SOFTEN TOO MUCH WHEN THEY COOK.

SERVES 4

Apricot sauce:
1 cup (6 ounces) no-soak dried
    apricots
2 cups (16 fluid ounces) orange
    juice

Fritters:
3 dessert apples, e.g., Baldwin,
    Cortland
All-purpose flour, to dust
Oil for deep-frying
1 quantity (1 to 1½ cups) Yeast
    Batter (see page 14)
1 teaspoon ground cinnamon
Pinch of ground nutmeg
2 teaspoons confectioners'
    sugar

1 To make the sauce, simmer the apricots and orange juice in a covered saucepan for 10 minutes or until the apricots are soft. Blend in a blender or food processor and dilute if necessary with extra juice.

2 To make the fritters, core the apples and peel if preferred. Cut the apples into ¼-inch rings and dust with flour.

3 Heat oil for deep-frying to 350°F. Stir the batter, dip the apple rings in it until coated, and fry 3 or 4 at a time until crisp and golden brown. Drain and sprinkle with the cinnamon, nutmeg, and confectioners' sugar. Serve with the warm sauce.

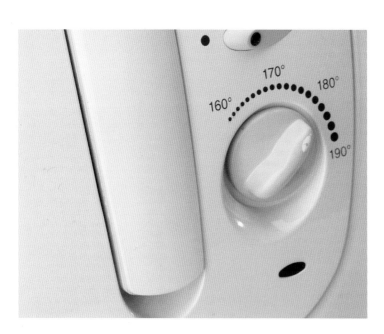

Apple Funnel Cakes ILLUSTRATED LEFT

COOK THESE IN A DEEP SKILLET OR OTHER WIDE PAN, POURING THE BATTER CAREFULLY INTO THE HOT OIL IN A SLOW STEADY STREAM FROM A TEAPOT.

MAKES 6

1¼ cups (5 ounces) all-purpose
    flour
1 teaspoon baking powder
¾ cup (6 fluid ounces)
    unsweetened apple juice
1 egg, beaten
1 teaspoon ground ginger
Oil for deep-frying
3 tablespoons superfine sugar

1 Sift the flour and baking powder into a bowl, make a well in the center, and gradually whisk in the apple juice, beaten egg, and half the ginger to make a smooth batter. Leave to stand for 1 hour. Add more water if the batter is too thick.

2 Pour one-third of the batter into a teapot or similar vessel. Heat about 1 inch of oil in a large skillet to 325°F and slowly pour batter into the oil in a tight spiral, approximately 6 inches in diameter. Fry for 3 to 4 minutes until golden brown, turning the spiral over after 2 minutes. Drain and fry the rest of the batter to make six cakes.

3 Mix the remaining ginger with the superfine sugar and toss the hot cakes in it. Serve warm with caramelized apple slices—melt ½ stick butter in a pan and sprinkle over 4 tablespoons superfine sugar, stirring until it dissolves. Add apple slices and cook until caramelized. Spoon over the apple cakes with the buttery juices in the pan.

Banana Fritters with Orange Cream

FRUIT FRITTERS ARE POPULAR IN THE WEST INDIES WHERE BOTH BANANAS AND SWEET SPICES LIKE NUTMEG AND CINNAMON ARE PLENTIFUL.

SERVES 6

Cream:
1 cup (8 fluid ounces) heavy cream
Rind of 1 orange, finely shredded

Fritters:
2 pounds ripe bananas (skins off)
2 eggs, beaten
½ teaspoon ground allspice
¼ teaspoon grated nutmeg
1 tablespoon muscovado sugar
2 teaspoons baking powder
Oil for deep-frying
Superfine sugar, to dust

1 To make the cream, whisk the heavy cream and orange rind together until standing in soft peaks. Spoon into a serving dish and chill until needed.

2 To make the fritters, peel and mash the bananas. Add the eggs, allspice, nutmeg, muscovado sugar, and baking powder and beat to form a thick batter.

3 Heat 1 inch oil in a large skillet and drop in small spoonfuls of the batter. Fry for 2 to 3 minutes until golden, turning over once.

4 Drain the fritters, dust liberally with superfine sugar, and serve warm with the cream.

Fruit Tempura with Raspberry Sauce

THE FRUIT NEEDS TO BE RIPE SO THE PITS CAN BE REMOVED EASILY BUT NOT TOO SOFT OR THEY
WILL BE DIFFICULT TO RE-SHAPE AROUND THE HAZELNUT FILLING.

SERVES 4

Raspberry Sauce:
1 pound raspberries
**½ cup (4 ounces) superfine
    sugar**

Tempura:
**¼ cup (1½ ounces) shelled
    hazelnuts**
1 tablespoon brown sugar
3 tablespoons cream cheese
6 red plums
6 apricots or yellow plums
**1 quantity (about 2 to 2½ cups)
    Tempura Batter (see page 14)**
Oil for deep-frying
All-purpose flour, to dust
**¼ teaspoon finely shredded
    nutmeg**

1 To make the sauce, simmer the raspberries and sugar
together until the fruit is soft. Blend and, if you prefer a
smooth sauce, push through a strainer to remove the seeds.

2 To make the tempura, finely chop the hazelnuts and mix
with the sugar and cream cheese.

3 Halve the plums and apricots, remove the pits and then
sandwich the halves back together with the hazelnut
mixture.

4 Make up the batter and heat oil for deep-frying to 375 °F.
Dust the fruit with flour, dip in the batter and fry 3 or 4 at
a time for about 3 minutes until golden and crisp.

5 Drain the tempura and serve with the warm sauce. Sprinkle
over the nutmeg.

Cinnamon Puffs with Blueberry Sauce

OTHER FRUITS COULD BE USED TO MAKE THE SAUCE SUCH AS BLACKCURRANTS, RASPBERRIES, OR APRICOTS. IF USING FRUIT THAT HAS BEEN CANNED OR BOTTLED IN SYRUP, OMIT THE SUGAR FROM THE RECIPE AND FOR LARGER FRUITS, BLEND THE SAUCE IN A BLENDER BEFORE ADDING THE ARROWROOT.

SERVES 6

Sauce:
2 cups (1 pound) blueberries
½ cup (4 fluid ounces) water
¼ cup (2 ounces) granulated sugar
Juice of 1 orange
1 tablespoon arrowroot or cornstarch

Cinnamon puffs:
1 cup (4 ounces) all-purpose flour
1 teaspoon ground cinnamon
⅔ cup (6 fluid ounces) water
2 ounces (½ stick) butter, cut into small pieces
2 medium eggs, beaten
Rind of ½ orange, finely shredded
1 tablespoon granulated sugar
Oil for deep-frying

To finish:
Fine shreds of orange rind
Granulated sugar, to dust

1 To make the sauce, simmer the blueberries, water, sugar, and orange juice together in a covered saucepan for 15 minutes or until the blueberries are soft, mashing them occasionally with a spoon. Mix the arrowroot with 2 tablespoons cold water and set aside.

2 To make the puffs, sift the flour and cinnamon onto a sheet of waxed paper. Heat the water and butter in a saucepan until the butter melts. Bring to a fast boil, remove from the heat, and tip in all the flour. Beat with a wooden spoon until the mixture forms a smooth ball that leaves the sides of the pan.

3 Cool for a few minutes, then beat in the eggs a little at a time with the orange rind and sugar.

4 Heat oil for deep-frying to 325°F. Drop teaspoonfuls of the mixture into the oil and fry in batches for 4 to 5 minutes until puffed and golden brown. Drain and keep warm in a low oven.

5 Stir the arrowroot, and mix into the sauce. Reheat gently over a low heat until the sauce thickens, stirring occasionally.

6 Serve the warm puffs sprinkled with orange rind and dusted with granulated sugar with the hot sauce spooned around.

Mango and Ice Cream Parcels

IT'S IMPORTANT TO WORK QUICKLY WHEN ASSEMBLING THE PARCELS SO THE ICE CREAM HAS NO TIME TO MELT. ALTHOUGH THEY NEED TO BE FRIED AND SERVED STRAIGHT AWAY, THE PARCELS CAN BE MADE AHEAD AND KEPT IN THE FREEZER UNTIL 10 MINUTES BEFORE FRYING. ONCE COOKED THEY HAVE TO BE SERVED IMMEDIATELY—LIKE A SOUFFLÉ, DINERS MUST WAIT FOR THEM, NOT THE OTHER WAY ROUND!

SERVES 6

2 ripe mangos
6 sheets of phyllo pastry,
    measuring roughly 7 x 12
    inches
1 egg white, lightly beaten
6 scoops of vanilla ice cream
Oil for deep-frying
Confectioners' sugar, to dust

1 Place a baking sheet in the freezer.

2 Peel the mangos and cut the flesh away from the pit. Chop the flesh into small pieces.

3 Lay a sheet of phyllo lengthways on the worktop and spoon one-sixth of the mango flesh at one corner about 2 inches from the edge. Brush the pastry edges with egg white and place a scoop of ice cream on top of the mango.

4 Working quickly, fold the pastry corner over the mango and ice cream and roll up the pastry around the filling, tucking in the side flaps and sealing the edges. As soon as you have assembled the parcel, place it on the baking sheet in the freezer.

5 Make five more parcels in the same way, transferring each one immediately to the freezer as soon as it is made.

6 Remove the parcels from the freezer 10 minutes before cooking. Heat oil for deep-frying to 375°F and fry the parcels two at a time for 2 minutes until golden brown, turning over halfway. Drain the first two parcels when they are cooked, dredge with confectioners' sugar and serve these before you fry the next batch.

Index